Beneath the Carob Trees · The Lost Lives of Cyprus

Beneath the Carob Trees

The Lost Lives of Cyprus

Photographs by Nick Danziger

Words by Rory MacLean

Previous pages:
Nicosia International, once the largest airport on Cyprus, has been abandoned for more than 40 years. The scene of some of the heaviest fighting in 1974, it lies within the United Nations controlled Buffer Zone that separates the island's two communities.

Contents

Introduction   13

The Process   29

Archaeological Phase   49

Anthropological Phase   111

Genetic Phase   147

Identification and return of remains   167

Afterword   189

Epilogue by the CMP Members   196

The United Nations has been proud to facilitate the Committee on Missing Persons' work with the support of the international community. The Committee is helping to build a sustainable and joint future in Cyprus. I hope this effort will also provide lessons for other post-conflict situations and anywhere families yearn to learn the fate of their loved ones.

BAN KI-MOON
Secretary-General of the United Nations

We honour the Committee on Missing Persons in Cyprus and we take pride in being the largest donor supporting its work. The Committee has recovered and identified the remains of many and helped hundreds of Cypriot families to close a long period of anguish and uncertainty. We hope that closure will bring healing and that healing will foster reconciliation.

JEAN-CLAUDE JUNCKER
President of the European Commission

Introduction

In 1960 Cyprus became an independent state after near-continuous foreign occupation since the time of the Pharaohs. But nationalistic forces were already at work sundering its two communities. Within three years the inter-communal struggle between Greek and Turkish Cypriots turned violent. Targeted murders sowed fear across the island. Internal and external forces further deepened the mistrust, culminating in a Greek-sponsored coup d'état, the subsequent intervention of Turkish troops in 1974 and the de facto division of Cyprus.

During those brutal and tragic years thousands of men, women and children went missing: plucked off buses, pulled out of shops and hospitals, executed in villages or killed in battle. Their remains were thrown into wells, buried in secret, unmarked graves or simply left in the battlefield. Over the next three decades, with virtually no communication between the two communities, the tragedy of the missing – and the suffering of the bereaved – was used to bolster contrasting, nationalistic narratives.

Since 1981 the Committee on Missing Persons (CMP) – established by agreement between the Greek Cypriot and Turkish Cypriot communities under the auspices of the United Nations – has been mandated to tackle this humanitarian tragedy. First, the CMP led the long negotiations that produced the official list of 2,001 missing persons. Then, over the last decade, it has undertaken more than a thousand excavations and exhumations across the island, recovering and identifying half of the missing and returning their remains to their families. This extraordinary bi-communal work has been carried out by a new generation of Cypriots determined to heal the wounds left open by their fathers and grandfathers. *Beneath the Carob Trees* chronicles their efforts and pays tribute to all those who labour to end the suffering of the bereaved, and to support reconciliation between the communities.

Time is of the essence. With the passing years relatives desperately waiting for information on the fate of their loved one, as well as witnesses whose cooperation is vital in locating burial sites, are passing away at an ever-increasing rate. For some it is already too late. One widow's gravestone reads, 'If you find my husband, please bury him next to me'. The identity and dignity of so many Cypriots – so cruelly snatched from them some 40 or 50 years ago – must be restored before it is lost forever.

Following pages:
A United Nations soldier opens a gate for blue berets to patrol deserted no-man's-land in old Nicosia, the last divided city in Europe. The UN Buffer Zone stretches 180 kilometres across the island and ranges in width from a few metres to more than six kilometres.

When fighting erupted, residents rapidly left their homes and workplaces, leaving behind their old lives and possessions. Within the demilitarised Zone nothing has changed for decades, while life goes on today on both sides of the wall.

STOP
NO PHOTOGRAPHY
UN AUTHORISED PERSONNEL
AND VEHICLES ONLY
ΑΛΤ
ΑΠΑΓΟΡΕΥΕΤΑΙ Η ΛΗΨΗ ΦΩΤΟΓΡΑΦΙΩΝ
ΕΙΣΟΔΟΣ ΜΟΝΟ ΓΙΑ ΠΡΟΣΟΠΙΚΟ
ΚΑΙ ΟΧΗΜΑΤΑ
ΤΩΝ ΗΝΩΜΕΝΩΝ ΕΘΝΩΝ
DUR
FOTOĞRAF ÇEKMEK YASAKTIR
YALNIZ BİRLEŞMİŞ MİLLETLER
PERSONEL ve ARAÇLARI

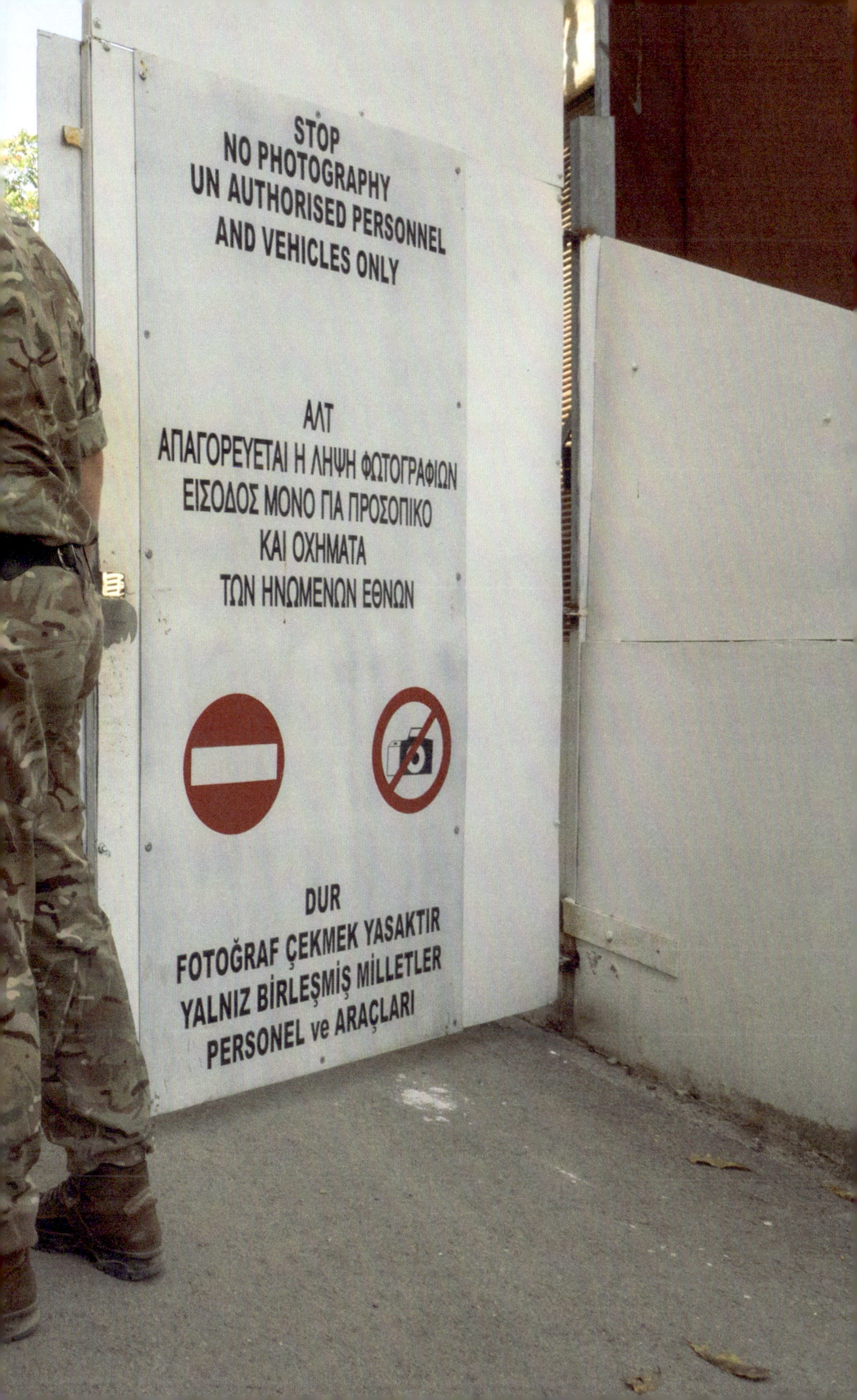

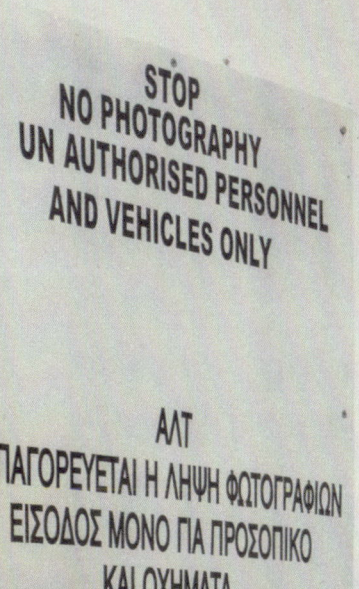

The Process

The primary objective of the CMP is to return the identified remains of missing persons to their families in order to arrange for a proper burial and close a long period of anguish and uncertainty. Each missing person case begins with an investigation into the circumstances of disappearance and possible location of remains. Once information on a possible burial site is obtained, the Committee's archaeologists conduct a meticulous excavation. If remains are found, these are exhumed and transported to the CMP Anthropological Laboratory for forensic analysis. Bone samples are taken for DNA extraction and matches are made to possible relatives. Once identification is confirmed, the remains can be handed over to the missing person's family for burial, with CMP psychologists providing emotional and practical support. At every stage of the exhumation and identification processes, teams of Greek Cypriot and Turkish Cypriot scientists work alongside each other.

Following pages:
Since 2006 the CMP has excavated 1,041 secret burial sites across the island. Every grave has been located by information gathered from witnesses of the murders, the perpetrators themselves, or their family and friends.

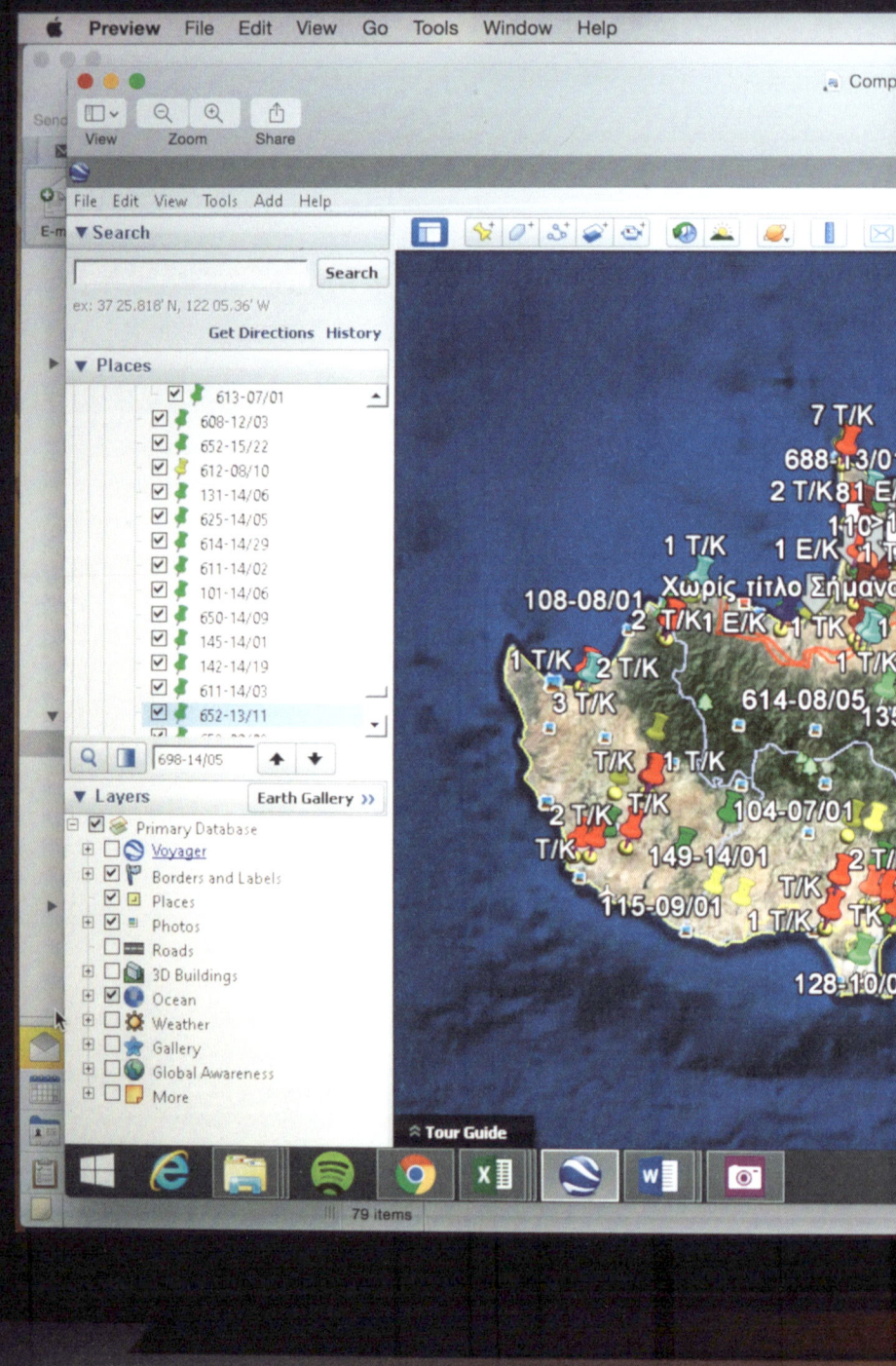

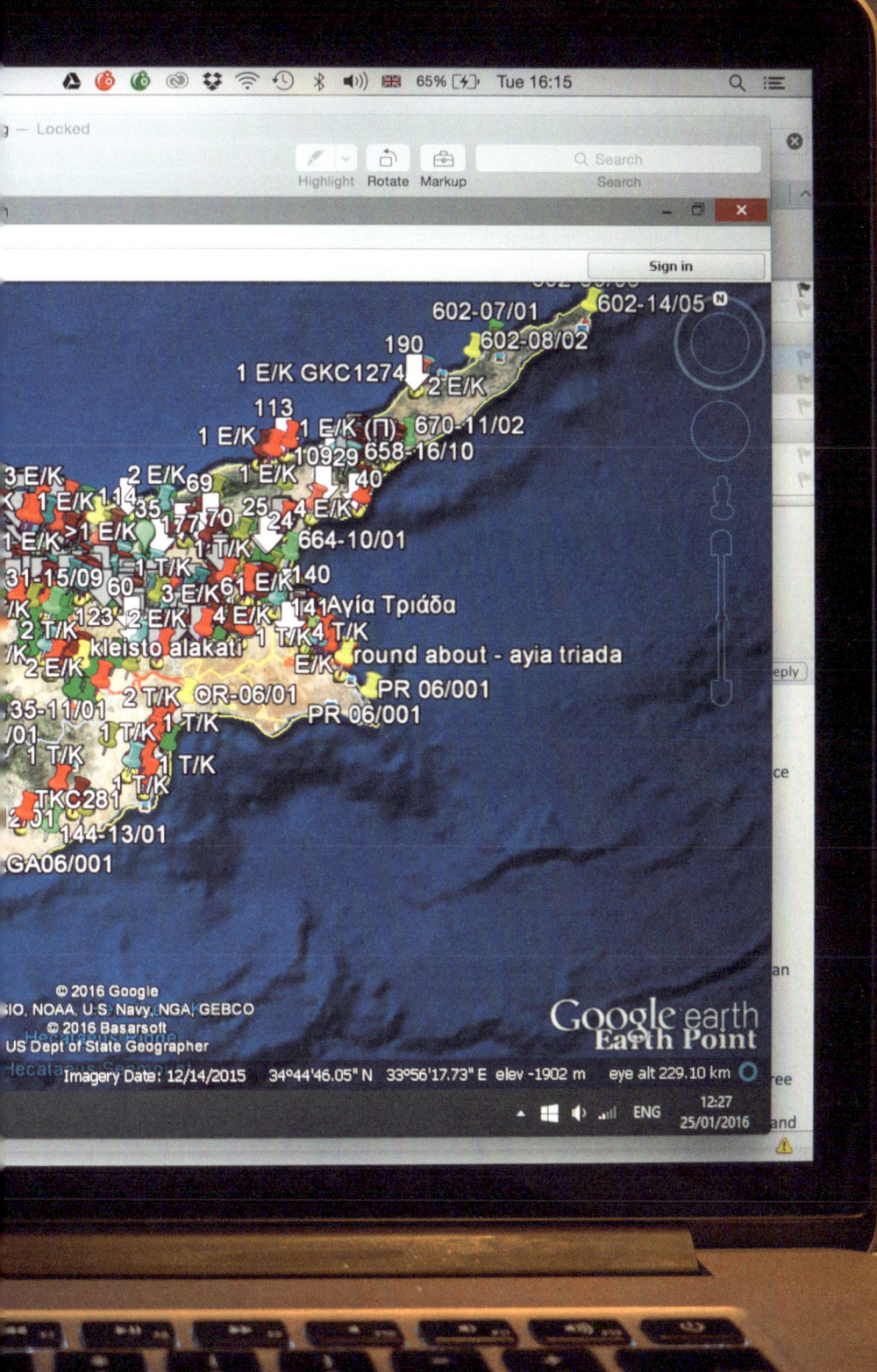

Murat Soysal, Assistant to the Turkish Cypriot Member of the Committee on Missing Persons, talks to a 95-year-old witness at her family farm. Her testimony enabled CMP archaeologists to find and exhume the remains of 36 missing persons. As elderly witnesses age and die, time is running out to find the remains of the thousand Cypriots who are still missing.

Murat Soysal

'I never take a notebook with me. I just listen. I am good at remembering stories.'

Every morning Murat Soysal, 41, sits at a melamine table in the CMP's streetside north Nicosia office and listens. He listens to the arriving investigators, listens to rumours, listens to another call on his mobile.

'Investigators are like the bow of a ship: where they lead the whole of the CMP follows,' he said in his softly spoken manner, sipping his coffee. Around him teams of young archaeologists noisily gathered tools and directions, lugged shovels and sunshades out of the open door to the rank of black, four-wheel-drive pick ups.

'In the early days it was dangerous for people to talk to us. Informants and witnesses were bullied into silence. Our investigators were threatened. The perpetrators feared being exposed, of course. But today they understand that our work is humanitarian, that the information is not used against them.'

Every investigation begins with a whisper. The CMP's seven Turkish Cypriot investigators – alongside Murat – follow leads, linger over coffees and listen for the truth. Their work is mirrored by Greek Cypriot investigators active in the south of the island. Sometimes the investigators coax witnesses into confession. Sometimes they rely on hearsay. Sometimes a murderer will reveal himself by blurting out on his deathbed, 'I killed him and buried him under a carob tree.' But most often perpetrators and primary witnesses alike will try to distance themselves from any killing, by insisting for example that they only heard the gunshots.

'They tell you yet they cannot tell you,' said Murat, a diplomatic and principled man. 'The missing persons project began because of a need. Citizens on both sides pressurised the politicians to act. "Help us to help them", we tell our informants.'

Sometimes an investigation can take years. Once Murat visited a suspect half-a-dozen times, bringing him small gifts, even arranging for his long-broken water main to be repaired. Yet every time the suspect insisted that he knew nothing about a certain murder, claiming that he'd been away in the mountains that day.

'But I'm not a quitter. I never accept defeat,' said Murat.

Then the man's elder brother died and Murat confronted him again. 'Let's cut the crap,' he told him after paying his condolences. 'I know your brother did the killing and you buried the corpse.'

'You are right. I'll show you where,' admitted the man.

On other occasions Murat and his investigators have been told – politely – to leave a village and never come back again.

'When we plan our investigations we choose the best apples in the basket,' he said. 'There are always some rotten apples.'

Over the last decade the remains of 470 Greek Cypriots have been found and identified in the north; 1,038 are still missing. In the south the remains of 148 Turkish Cypriots have been found and returned to their families, out of 493 missing persons.

Like many Turkish Cypriots, Murat's parents had moved to the north in 1974, the year of his birth. In the south they'd left behind a small two-room house with an attached workshop where his mother had worked as a seamstress.

'As a kid I often stared across the border and wondered why the island was divided. In time I understood and – when the gates opened in 2003 – I went for the first time to my family's old house in the south, in Kofinou. You will not believe this but – even though I had never been there – I recognised it immediately. It was as if it were part of my memory. I knocked on the door but the new occupant would not let me inside. That's how it is,' he shrugged with a sad smile. 'My family suffered through very difficult times but we are one of the luckiest families in Cyprus. "Lucky" because none of our relatives was killed or went missing.'

Their new home in Nicosia had once been owned by Greek Cypriots. One day Murat discovered that family's old photographs hidden in a corner cupboard.

'I've hidden them because they are precious to that family,' his mother admitted to him. 'These are memories that can't be lost. I believe that they will come back for them one day.'

Later Murat's mother asked the United Nations to find the original owners and return the photographs to them.

Murat won a place at the Turkish Maarif College in Nicosia and then Famagusta's Eastern Mediterranean University. He set his sights on diplomatic service and went on to complete his Masters at the University of Westminster. On his return to Cyprus he worked as foreign editor at *Kıbrıs*, the largest circulation newspaper in the north, and then in the commercial sector. In 2003 he was hired as a Third Secretary to serve in one of the overseas representation offices of the Turkish Cypriot community.

He was ecstatic but realistic. He knew that a lowly Third Secretary would not be appointed to any of the more exotic locations abroad. Then he happened to meet a Turkish fortune-teller.

'I don't believe in second sight. I told her that all she did was fool innocent people. So she asked if I'd let her try on me.'

Murat agreed, letting her read the grains in his coffee cup.

'I see the Statue of Liberty,' the woman told him. 'You will live in New York.'

Six months later he was posted to the Manhattan office.

'I'd introduce myself as Deputy Representative, and then point out that only two diplomats worked in our office,' he recalled with a laugh.

On his return to Cyprus four years later Murat was offered the post of Assistant to the Turkish Cypriot Member of the Committee on Missing Persons. He took off his suit and tie and put on jeans and a t-shirt and set to work in local cafés and at suspected gravesites, helping to guide and direct the CMP's operations, planning excavations and – above all – listening.

'The families of the missing have only us,' he said. 'No one else helps them to find their missing. It's for them that we want to discover the truth, to find the missing and to give them a grave so that they can have closure. No human deserves to remain missing.'

Beyond an industrial estate to the north of the capital stands an earthen brick and breezeblock family farm. Its half-dozen outbuildings crumble and collapse into the dust. Two scrawny sheep grazed around a century-old plough. A single chicken pecked at the legs of an armchair.

'On my wedding day my husband and I were given ten sheep,' remembered its 95-year-old widowed owner. 'At its peak we had 500 sheep.'

In 1974 the woman had spotted newly disturbed soil at the edge of her 'rabbit food field'. Then armed men had spotted her. They'd chased her but she'd managed to escape and hide. She had kept her secret hidden for more than four decades, until last year when Murat had found her. Now he returned to the farm to pay his respects, and to thank her for helping to bring about the recovery of 20 missing Cypriots.

Murat squatted beside her. Her watery, lidless eyes gazed out from a sun-blistered face peppered with age spots. Her bone-thin arms seemed to be covered by little more than thin parchment. As he talked the widow held her walking stick in her hands. Informants are never paid for information yet when he finished she volunteered in a voice hardly louder than a whisper, 'You know, there is another mass grave...'

'I felt my hairs stand on end,' Murat said later that day,

brushing his arm. 'She told me about a certain dry riverbed. We had dug there before but never found the right spot. We have to work on this new information.'

Over the following weeks 16 more bodies were recovered from the new burial spot that the widow had identified.

'Cyprus is a most beautiful island where Cypriots have suffered over the years and are looking for a means to live together,' said Murat Soysal, an energetic and quietly confident diplomat. Often witnesses only come forward after the death of a family or village elder. Some witnesses also come forward in their dying days.

Xenophon Kallis, Assistant to the Greek Cypriot Member of the CMP, kneels at the edge of a recently-discovered mass grave.

Xenophon Kallis

Xenophon Kallis seems to hold the island's memory in his head.

'There are two types of killers,' he said, running a hand through his silver hair. 'First is the ideological killer who wants to change the world: to create a caliphate in Syria, to impose democracy on Iraq. He kills for his country, for his religion, for whatever. In time, with reflection, he comes to realise that he has done wrong and tries to hide away his deed like a naughty child. Yet he needs a catharsis, he needs the opportunity to confess to his wrongdoing.'

Xenophon paused, topped up his glass and went on, 'Second is the pathological killer. He is different, especially if he is of mixed blood. He kills to prove his loyalty to his community. A gun makes him macho. Killing earns him respect and status. Politicians across the globe draw people like him in from society's fringes, using them to achieve political ends. These killers do not regret their actions, for doubt – or any confession of wrongdoing – would negate their raison d'être.'

For almost 30 years Xenophon has cared for the missing of Cyprus, looking for information to establish their fate. On countless evenings, in hundreds of cafés, in thousands of hushed conversations, he has drawn the truth out of men and women from both communities.

'We are a small society so wherever we go, people know us.

And wherever we go, there is blood and murder.'

Xenophon's work is a calling, not a job. In many ways he is the conscience of the CMP.

'When a person goes missing, their identity is negated. They are denied both life and the right to be dead. This is barbarism. I try to convince the killers that their victims have a right to be brought back into society.'

Xenophon's childhood was 'filled with bloodshed'. He was born in 1951 in Dali, a mixed village close to Nicosia. He grew up in the long shadow of colonialism, not least after the British briefly imprisoned his left-wing parents. He remembers his first sight of a blue beret in 1964 – a Canadian UN peacekeeper – outside his school.

'I also remember Hussein Buba,' he volunteered. 'When I was a boy in Dali there were not many cars. Our neighbour Hussein Buba was the village bus driver. He was a kind man with a big moustache and gold teeth. Lots and lots of gold teeth. In 1963 paramilitaries stopped his bus, and asked who on board were Turkish Cypriots. Hussein Buba smiled his big golden smile and was taken off the bus. He was never seen again.'

Xenophon went on, 'I don't believe in metaphysics but a few years ago some remains of Turkish Cypriots found in Nicosia couldn't be identified. So I asked the scientists if the deceased had gold teeth. And he did. "This is Hussein Buba who used to drive me to school," I said to them. The DNA check confirmed that it was him.'

Through Xenophon's efforts, and those of Murat Soysal and other investigators, missing Cypriots have been unearthed from under new swimming pools, in cemeteries, at the bottom of Ottoman wells, in stone-clad lime kilns and hidden vehicles and beneath wild rubbish dumps under discarded asbestos.

'Even the tiniest fragment of bone has significance because its identity enables that missing person to be reincorporated into their society,' he said. 'It helps to restore a family's dignity. Also for me our work has created the opportunity to talk to both the Turkish Cypriots and the Greek Cypriots who were involved in the crimes, and this helps to give me hope for the future.'

Xenophon is a genuinely moral man. He radiates an infectious enthusiasm for life. He is convinced of the inherent goodness of the individual, even 'the biggest capitalist'. He is also gregarious and sparklingly intelligent. Unshaven and wearing a loose white shirt, he is prone to quote Marx and Che Guevara.

In contrast his office is a dark and cluttered place, crammed with files, books and maps of the divided island. Against one wall stands a print of Picasso's *Guernica*. The room is almost like the subconscious of Cyprus, with a makeshift altar assembled from small coffins at its centre. On it rest a few small bags of soil. When bones are returned, a family is also given a handful of earth from the spot where their father, mother, sister or son had died.

'I communicate with the killers by finding common ground,' Xenophon said. 'We have a drink together. We shoot the breeze.

Alcohol helps to break the chains. I try to establish a relationship based on trust, which I will never betray even though I disagree with almost everything the killer says. I try to break his loyalties to brother, to army, to country, to nationality. I offer to relieve him of the burden of guilt. As a result, in time, most killers will reveal things that they have never said to anyone.'

Xenophon – like Murat – is blessed with a prodigious memory. He can recall the details of almost every missing person, every killing field, every weeping widow on the island. As the CMP's leading Greek Cypriot investigator, he feels 'a moral responsibility to suffer with the sufferers'.

'People went missing in Cyprus for a political objective. Everyone knows what happened. Everyone knows that without truth and justice there cannot be peace and reconciliation. You can't make an omelette without breaking eggs. But none of the parties will admit publicly to murder, or allow themselves to be taken to court. In Cyprus the only logic is found in the contradictions. But wherever you are, you simply have to make the best of things.' He sighed, 'Life is like a plot of ground. On it you can grow the most beautiful flowers or poisonous weeds. I've had enough of the poison.'

'We are a small society so wherever we go, people know who we are. Wherever we go, there is blood and murder,' said Kallis in his office surrounded by files and coffins. 'Our work is hard. It's intense and sometimes dangerous. I've been, like others, threatened dozens of times. But all of us continue believing that what we are doing is right for the families and for peace in our country.'

Archaeological Phase

Exhumations are carried out across the island by 55 Cypriot archaeologists. These bi-communal teams excavate potential burial sites, guided by information gathered by the CMP investigators or received from other sources. When human remains are found, they are recovered by hand using meticulous archaeological techniques. Each step of the process is documented in photographs, detailed sketches and site maps, and all findings are labelled with unique identifying anonymous codes. Once the remains are exhumed, the Minimum Number of Individuals (MNI) buried in the particular gravesite is determined, based on the most repeated skeletal element. This number may, or may not, increase as a result of anthropological and genetic analyses.

Often burial sites are found to have been disturbed by natural processes – for example erosion – or human intervention. Occasionally remains are found to have been relocated intentionally from a primary burial site. In such cases, it is not always possible for the CMP to return a complete set of remains to the families.

Following pages:
A visiting Argentinian forensic specialist uses ground penetrating radar to detect hidden and overbuilt burial sites, in this case a suspected well with one or several corpses beneath the newly-paved Nicosia–Famagusta highway on the Mesaoria plain.

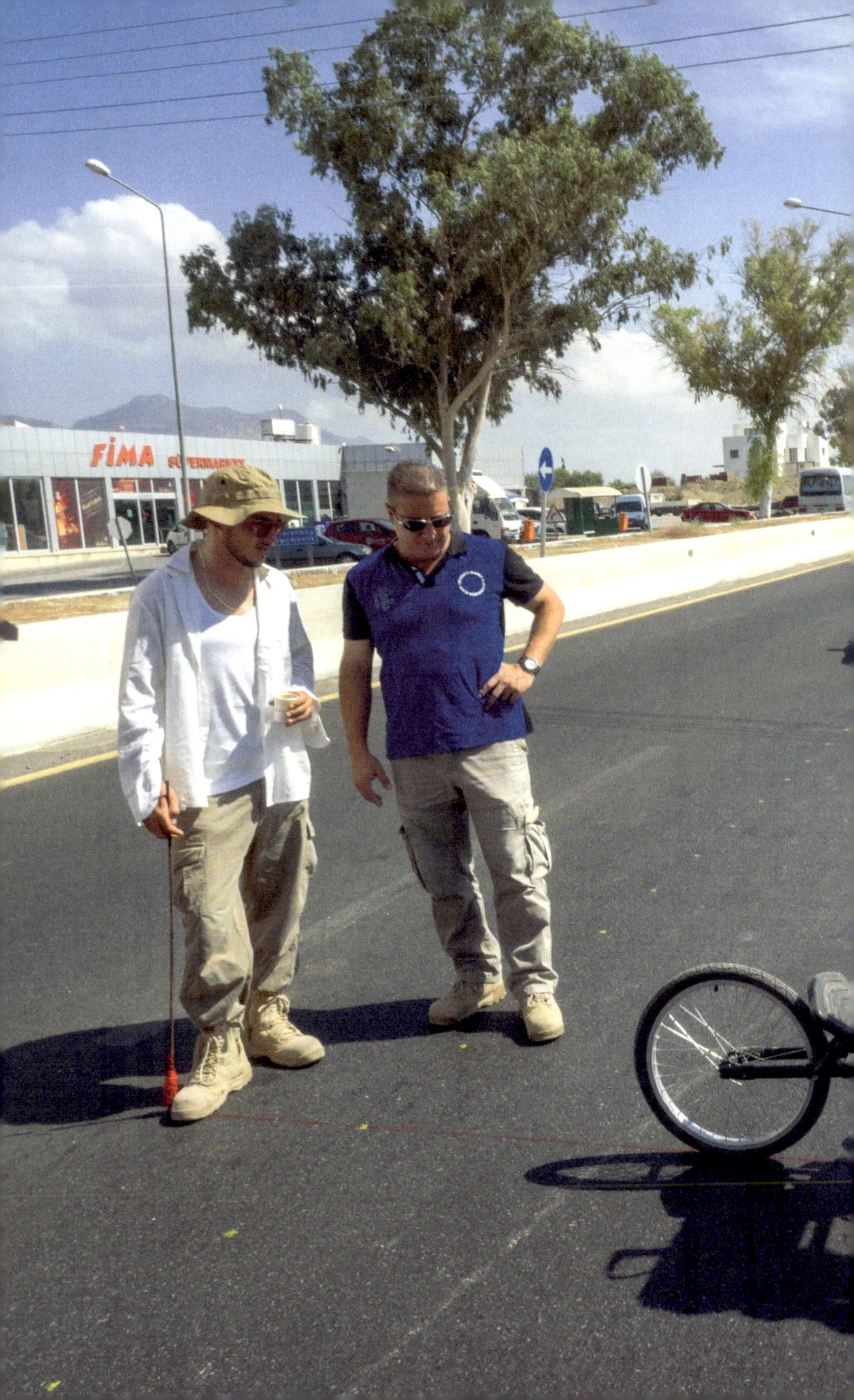
FİMA

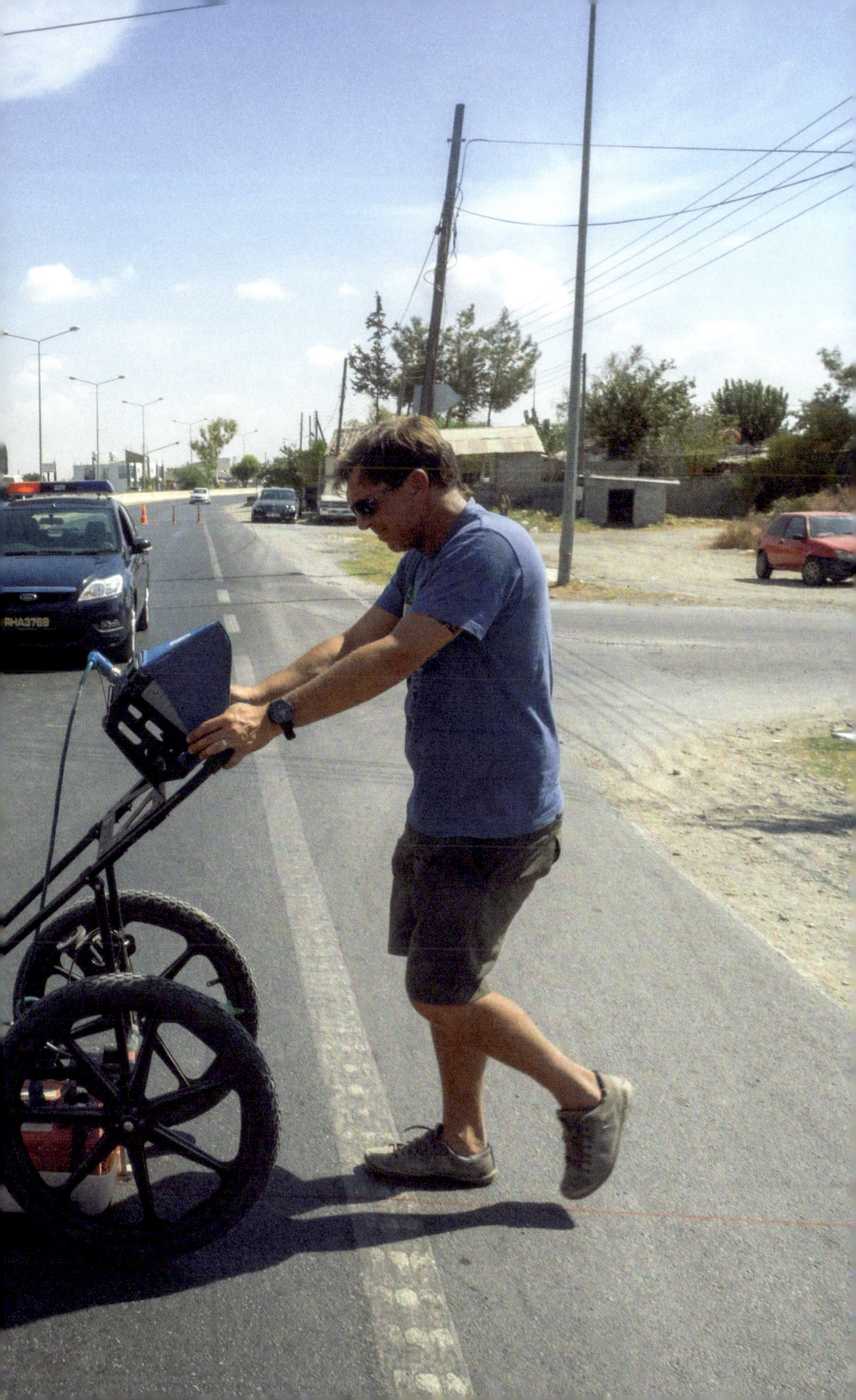

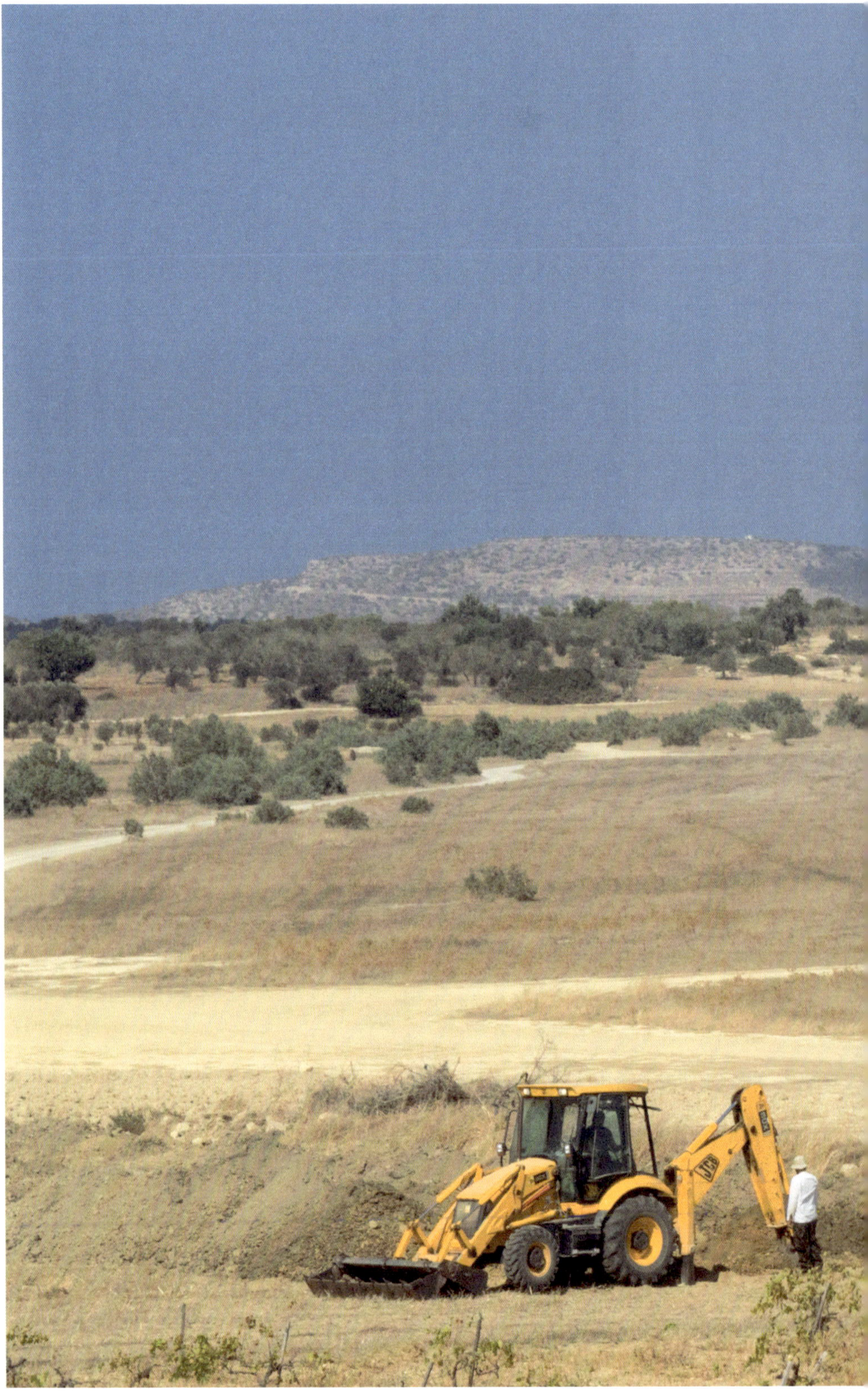
JCB

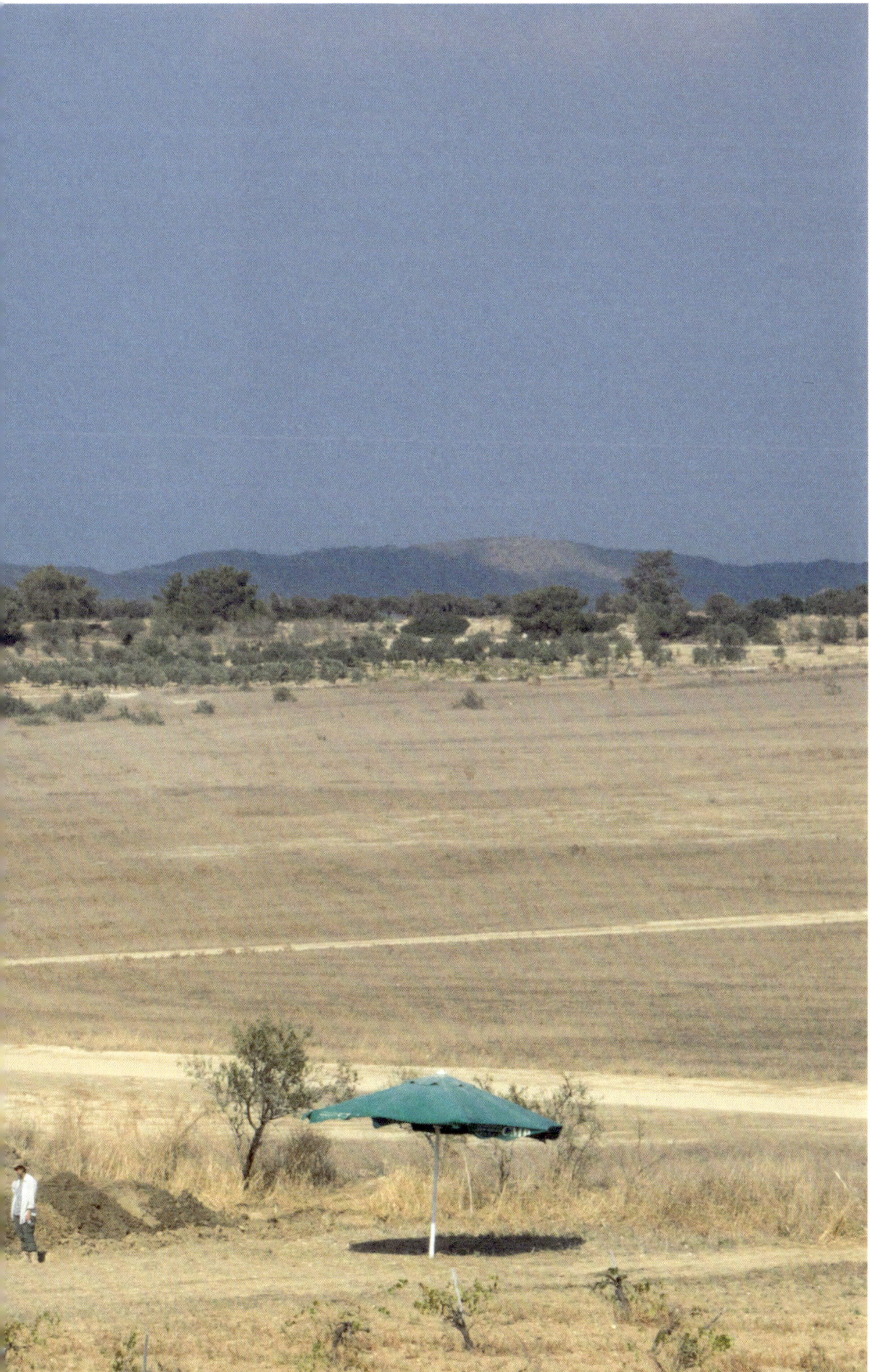

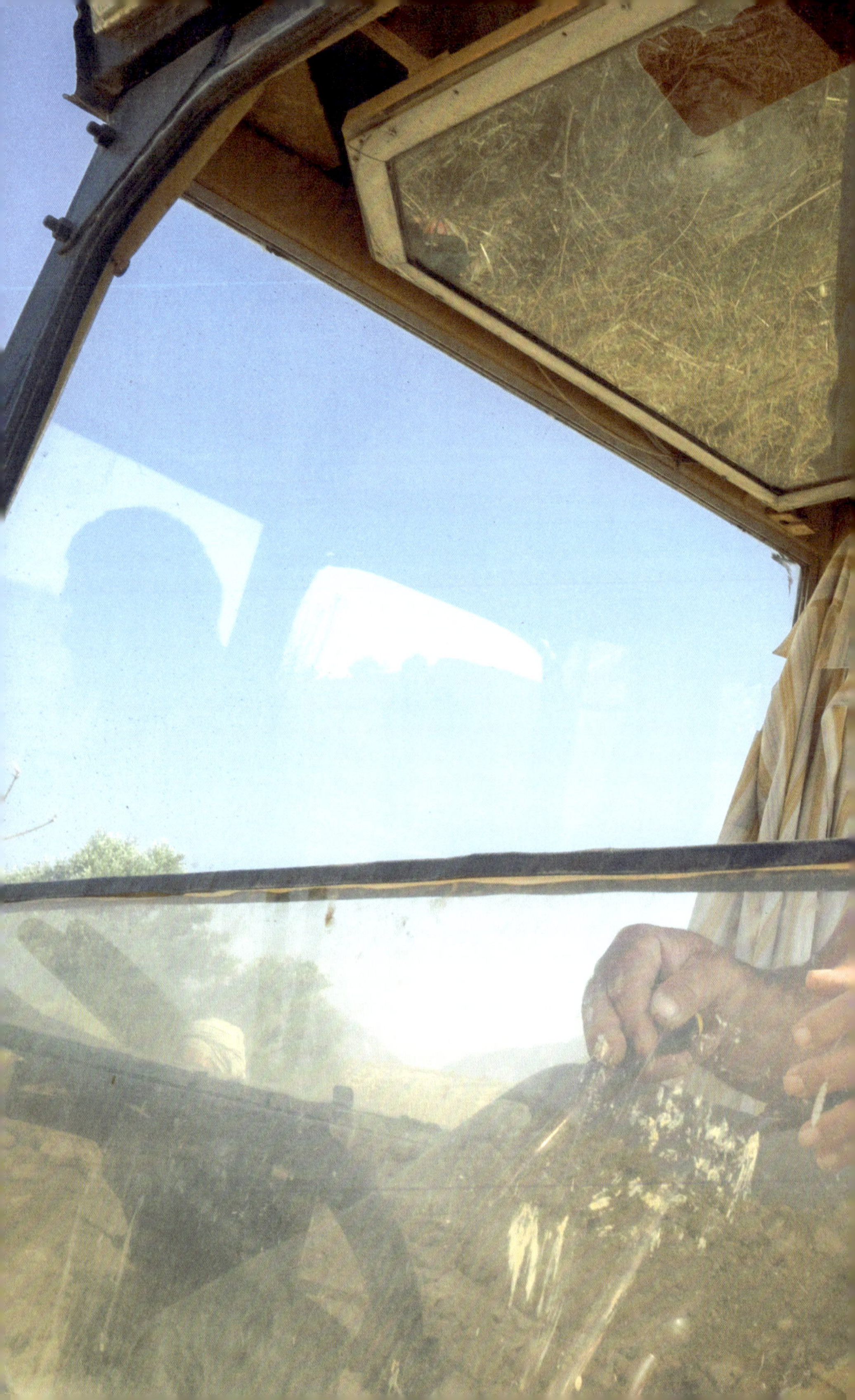

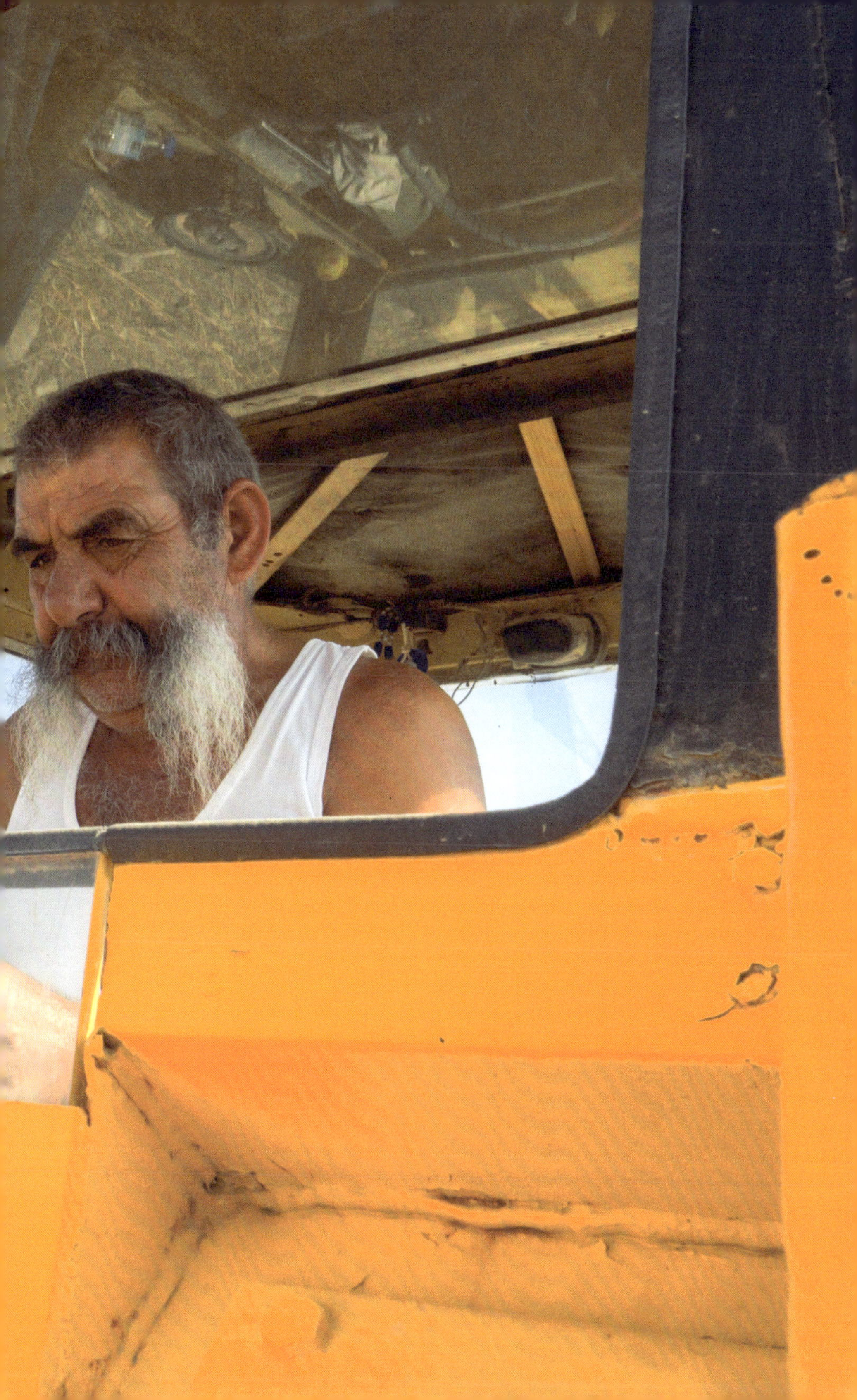

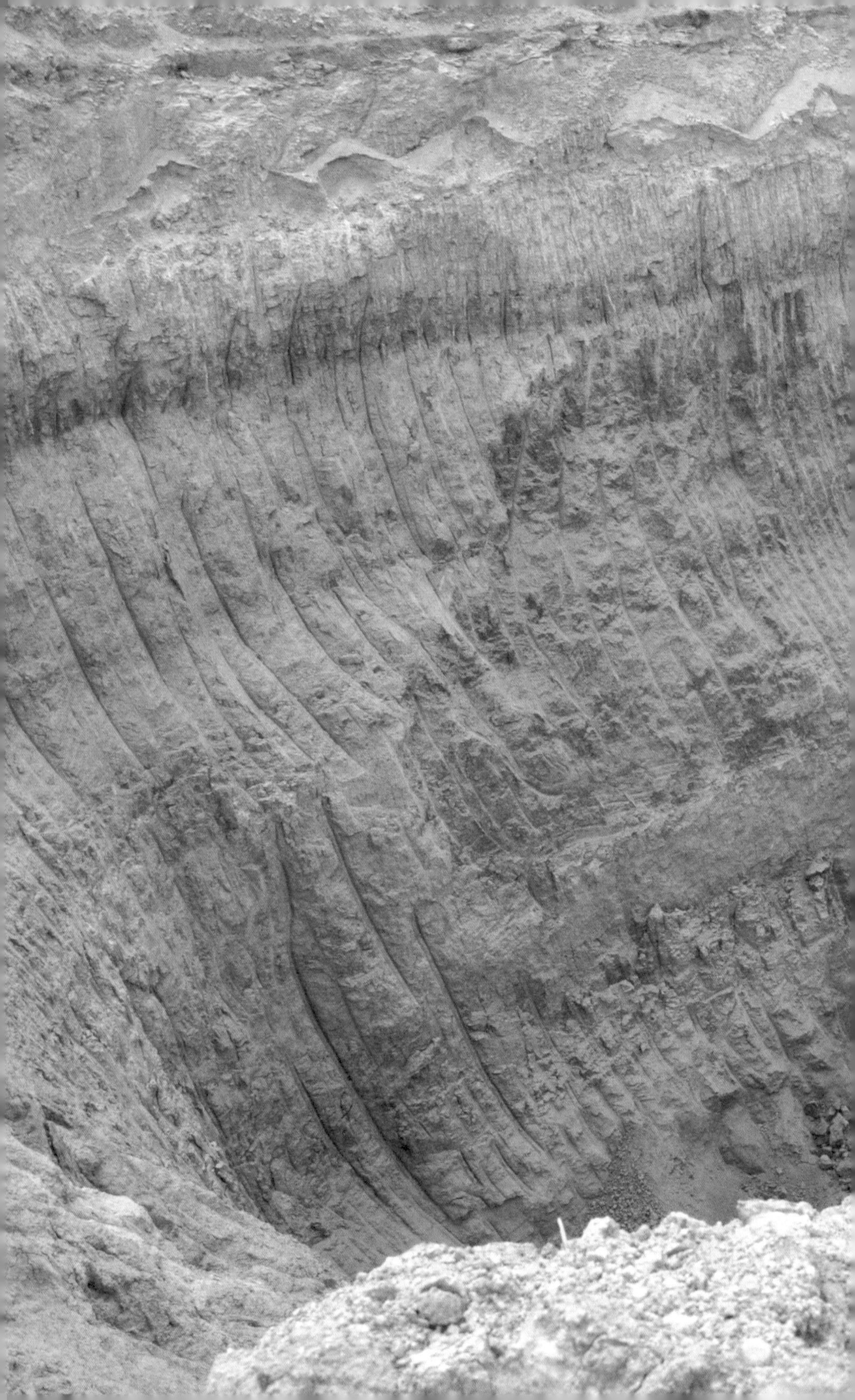

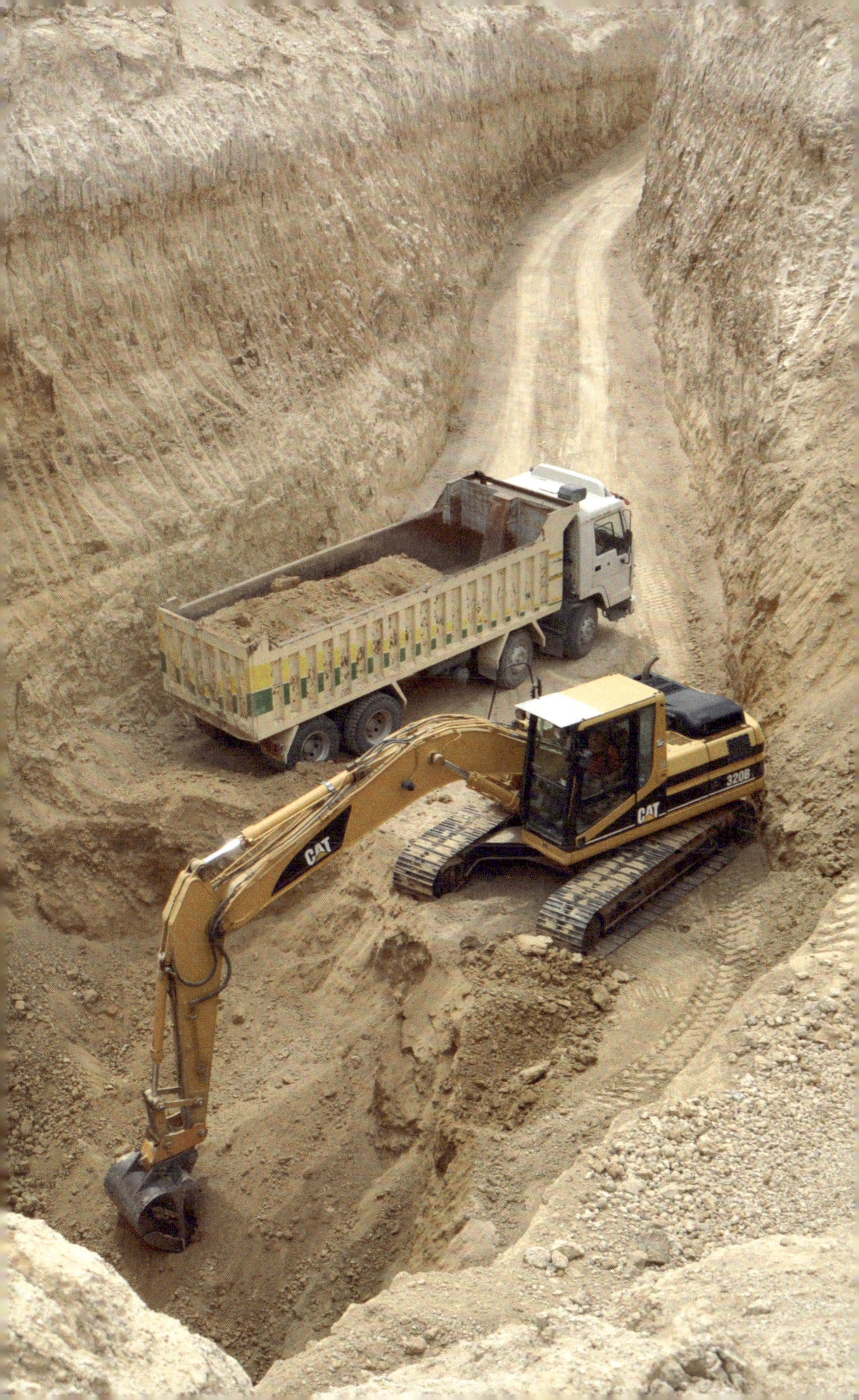
CAT
320B
CAT

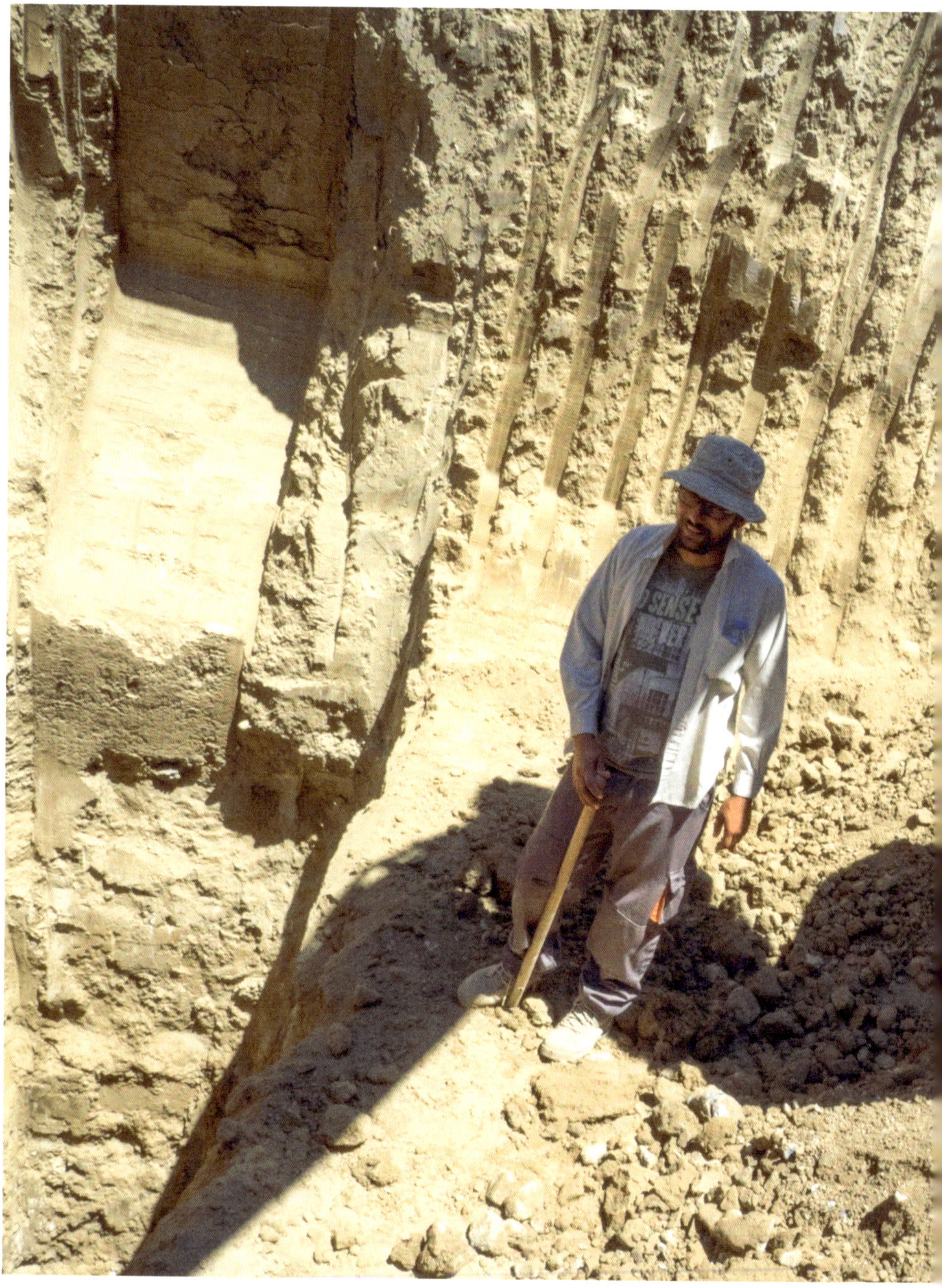

Previous pages:
A team of archaeologists excavate a suspected gravesite in 45°C summer heat. Like all members of the CMP, they work to recover and identify the missing and to return their remains to their families, in an effort to end the years of anguish and uncertainty.

Often the bodies of victims of killings were dumped into disused water wells. Decades on, the CMP reaches the well bottoms by digging ramps deep into the earth. After six months work at this site, the remains of one missing person was found at a depth of 31 metres.

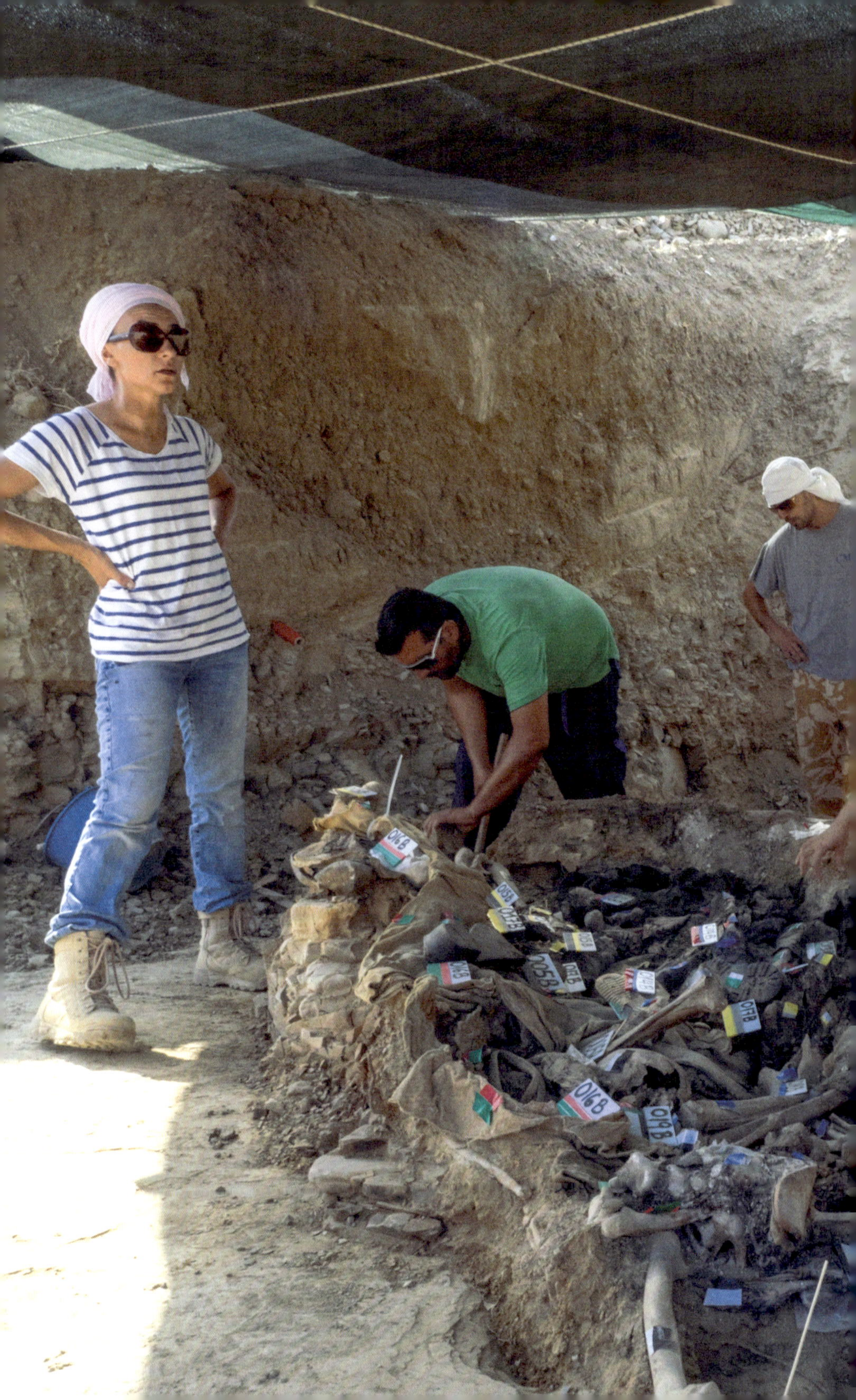

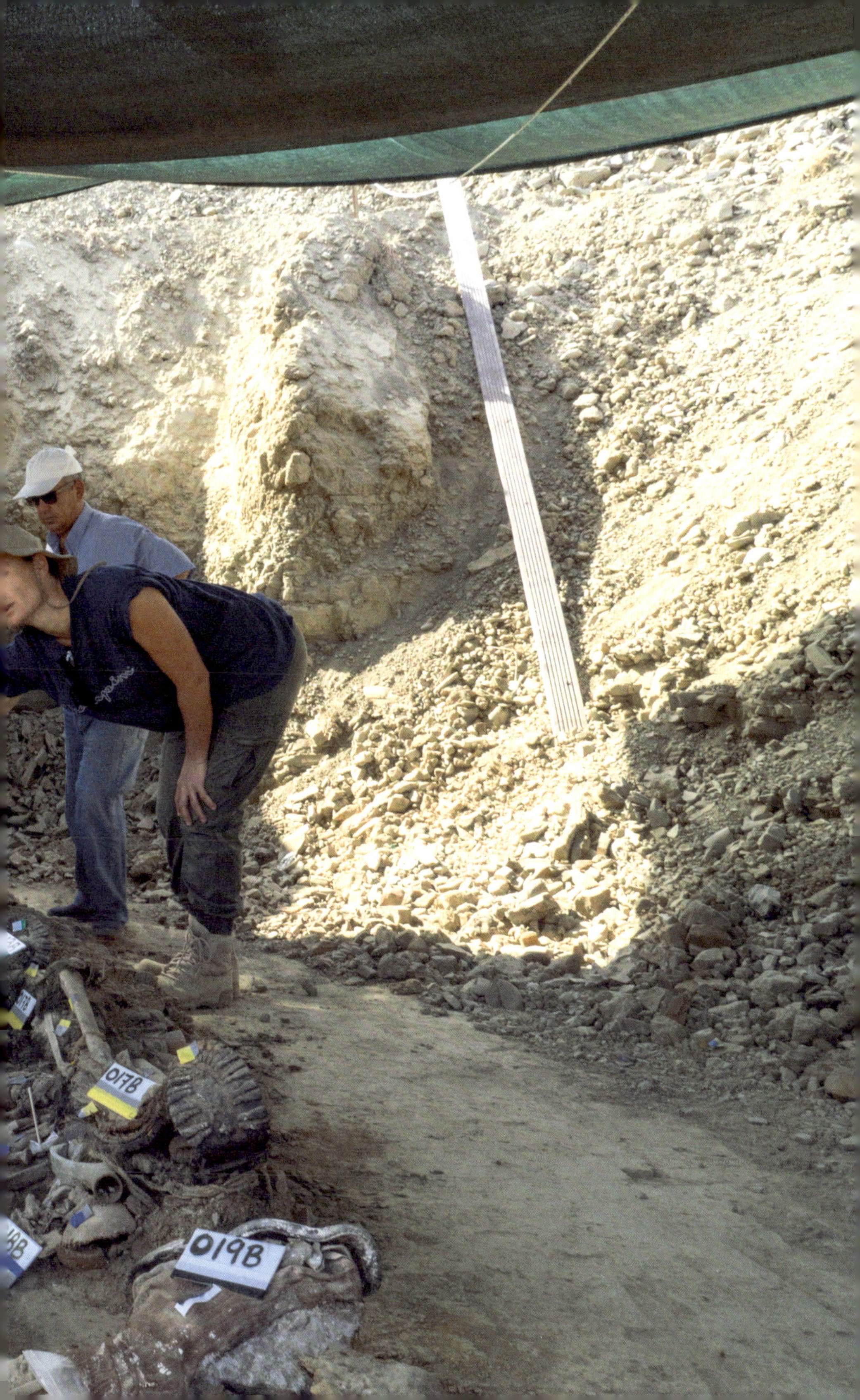
017B
019B

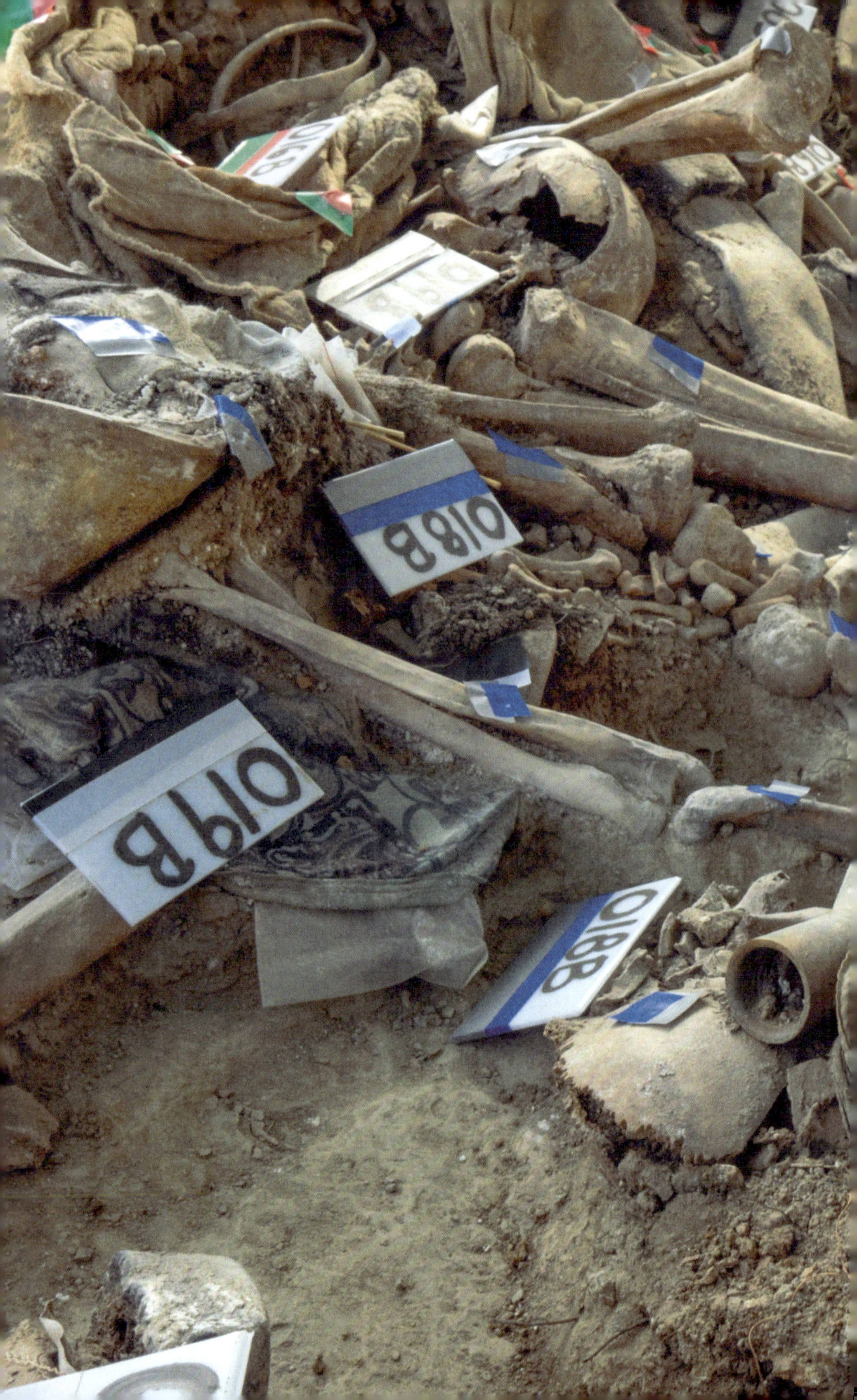

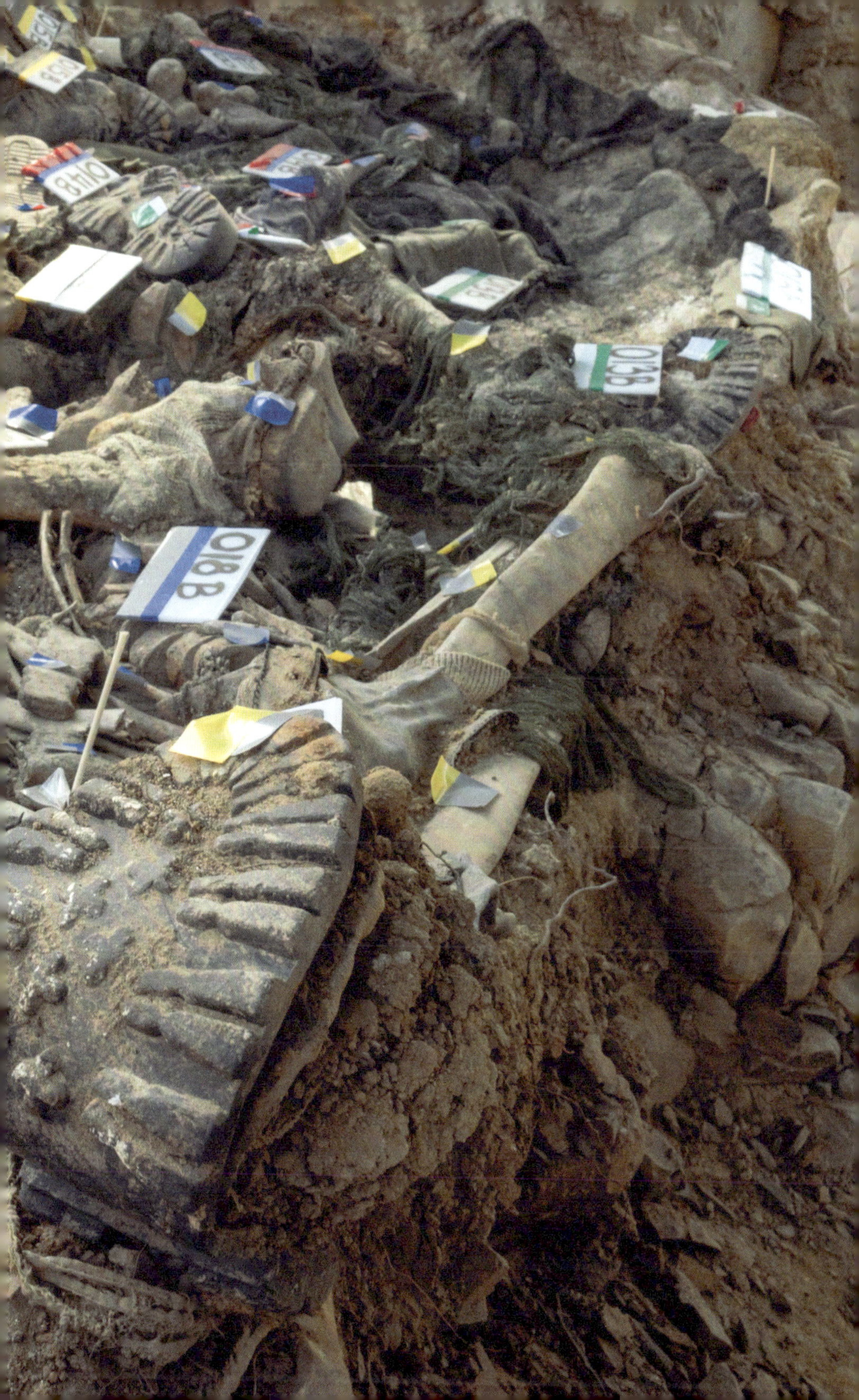

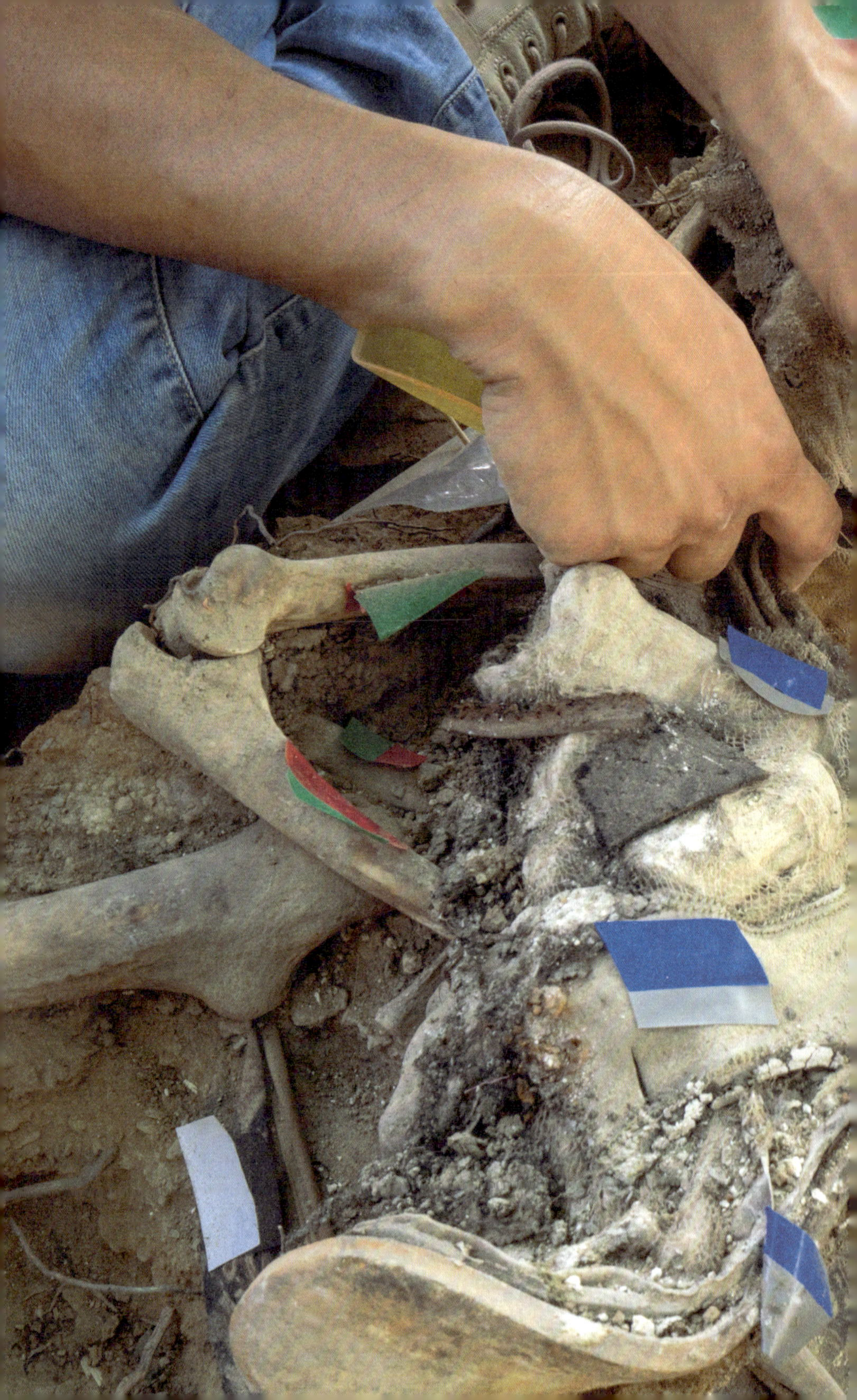

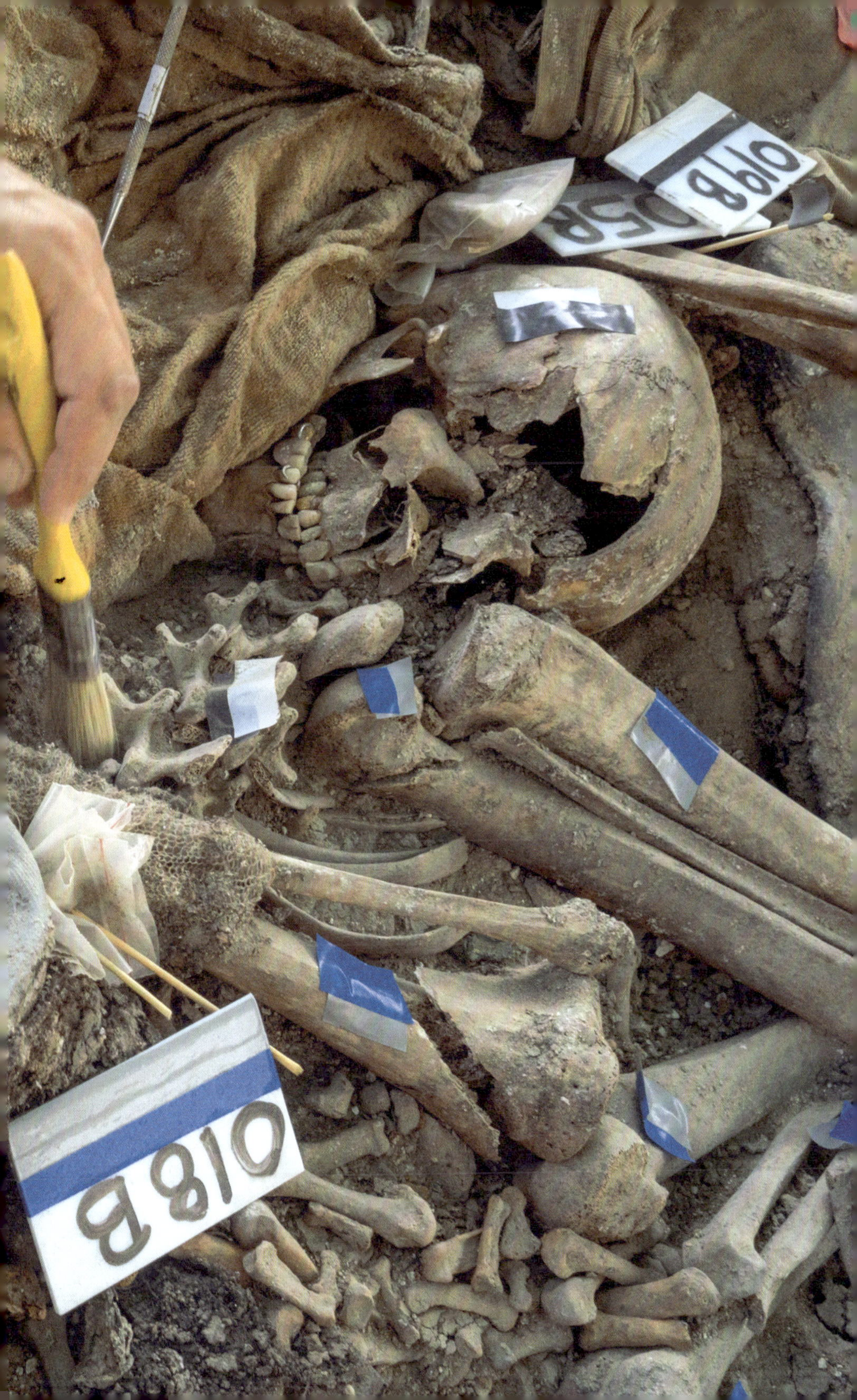
018B

Often weeks, even months, are needed to exhume and separate commingled remains. Strict forensic procedures are followed to distinguish each individual and ensure that there is no possibility of misidentification.

Following pages:
Most people who went missing in Cyprus were shot. Yet exhumation sites are not considered to be crime scenes. In line with its mandate, the CMP does not attribute responsibility for the deaths of any missing person or make findings as to the cause of such deaths, so as not to dis-courage further witnesses from coming forward to identify more graves.

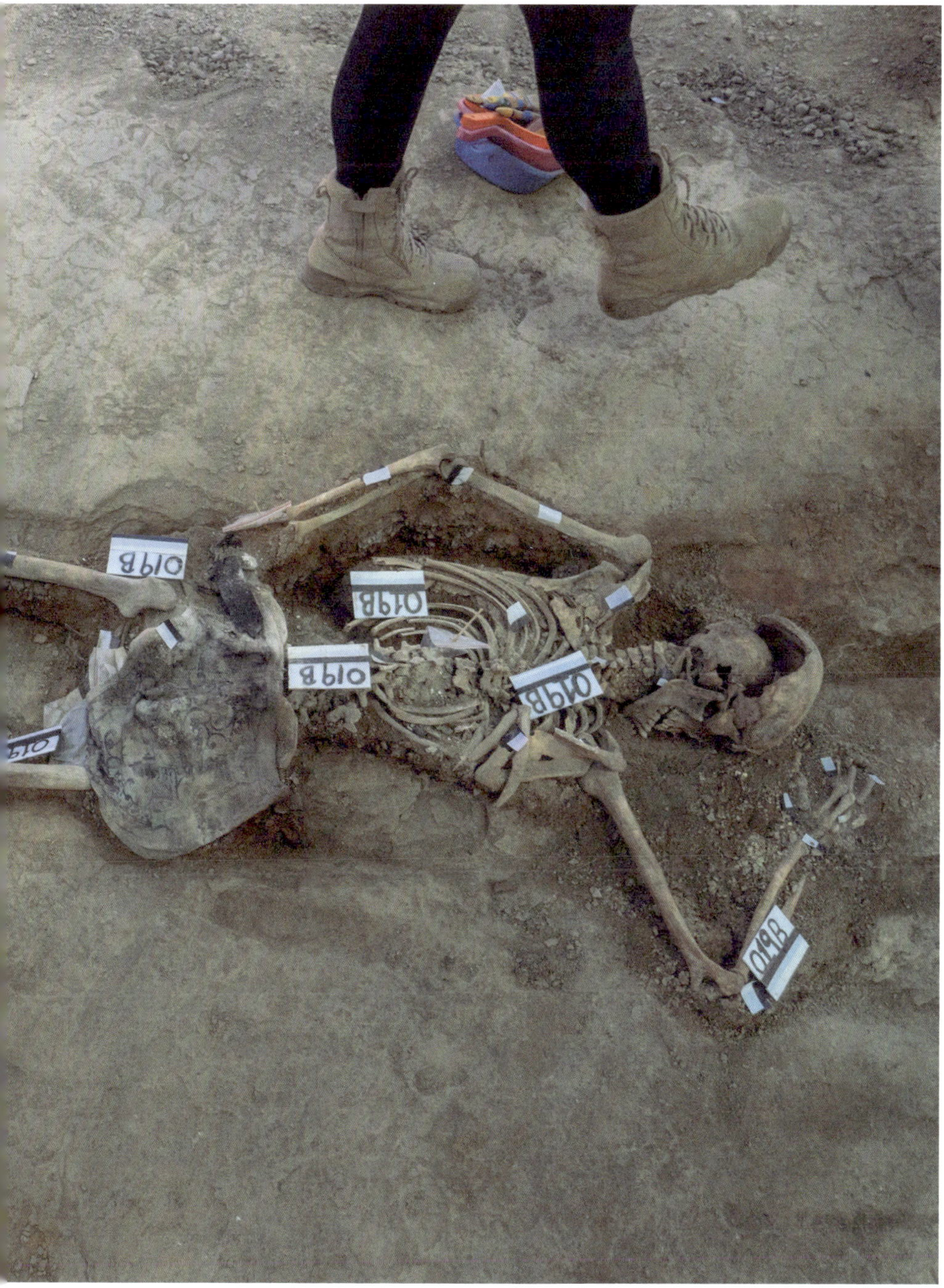
019B
019B
019B
019B
019B
019B

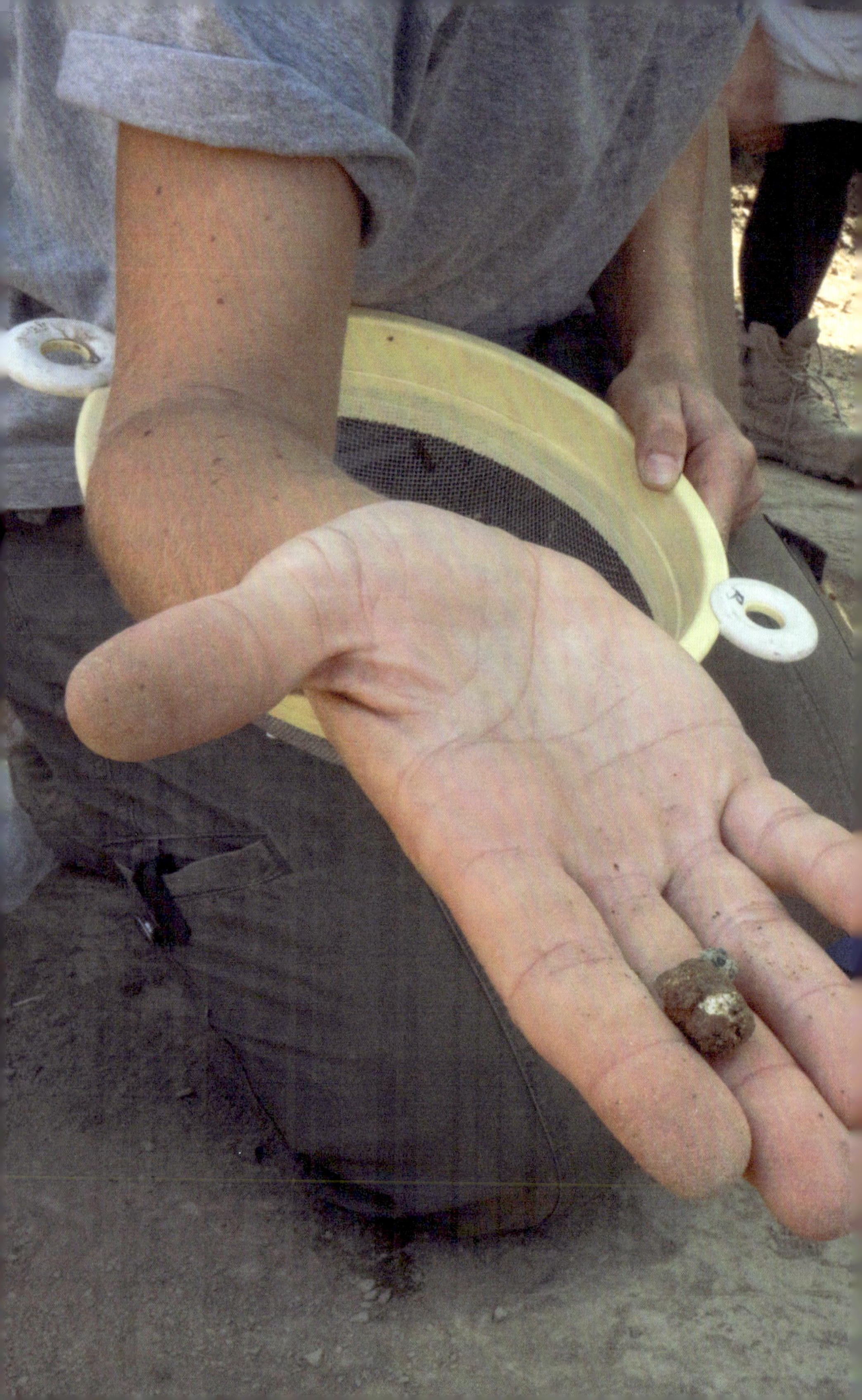

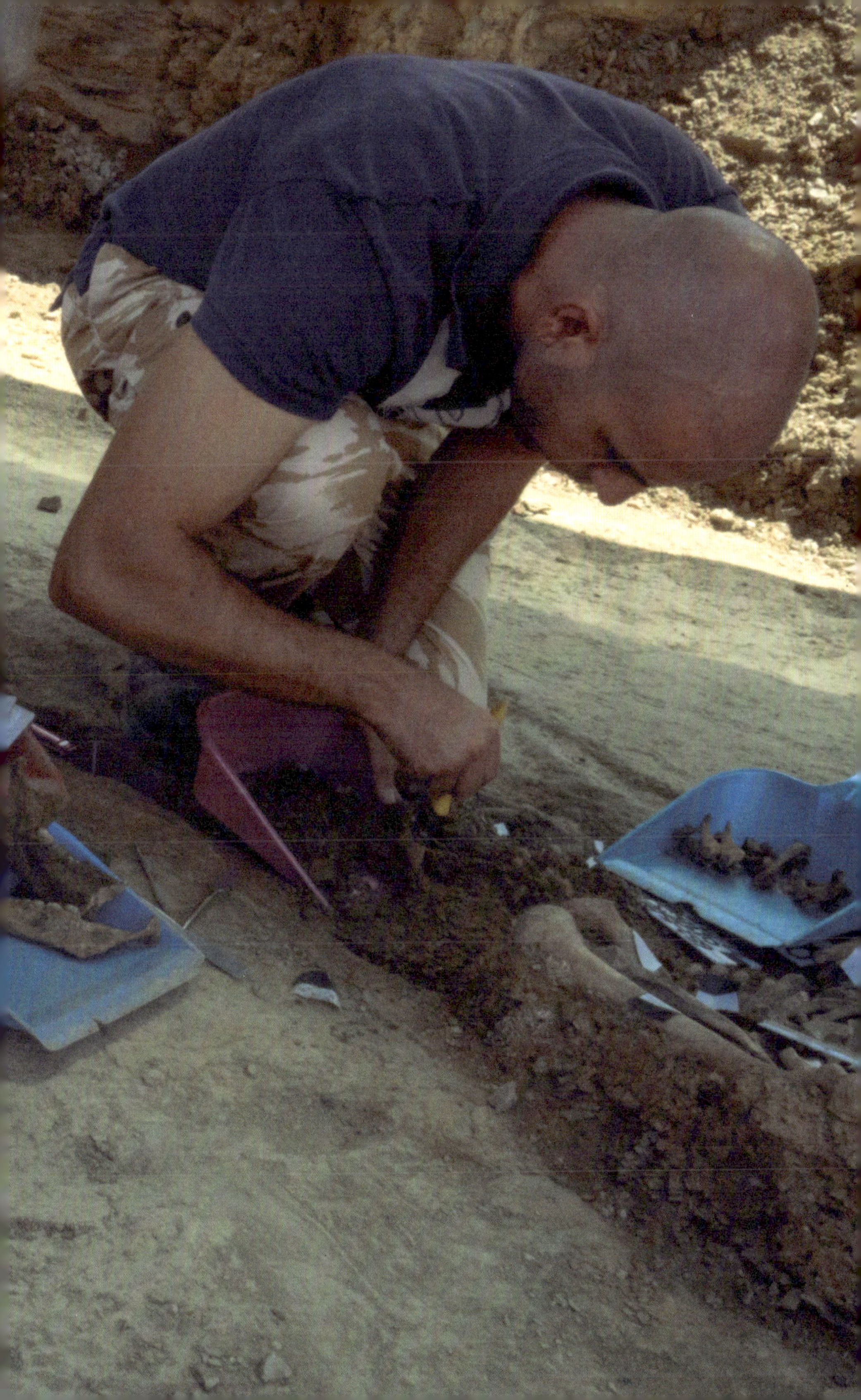

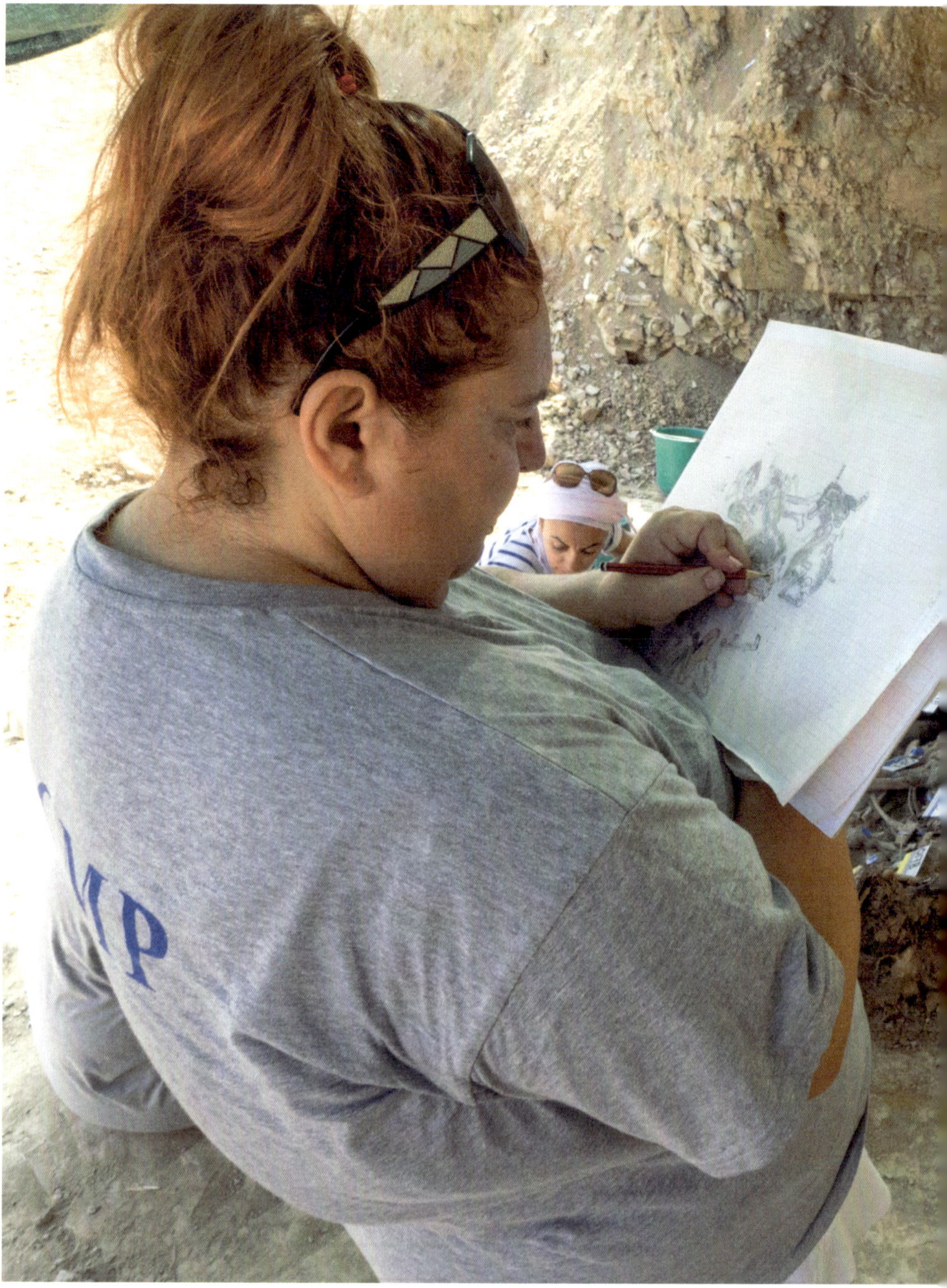

Every stage of excavations is recorded with photographs and drawings. Often possessions found alongside the remains – watches, wallets, rings and shreds of clothing – provide the most moving indicator of the victim's identity and individuality.

71

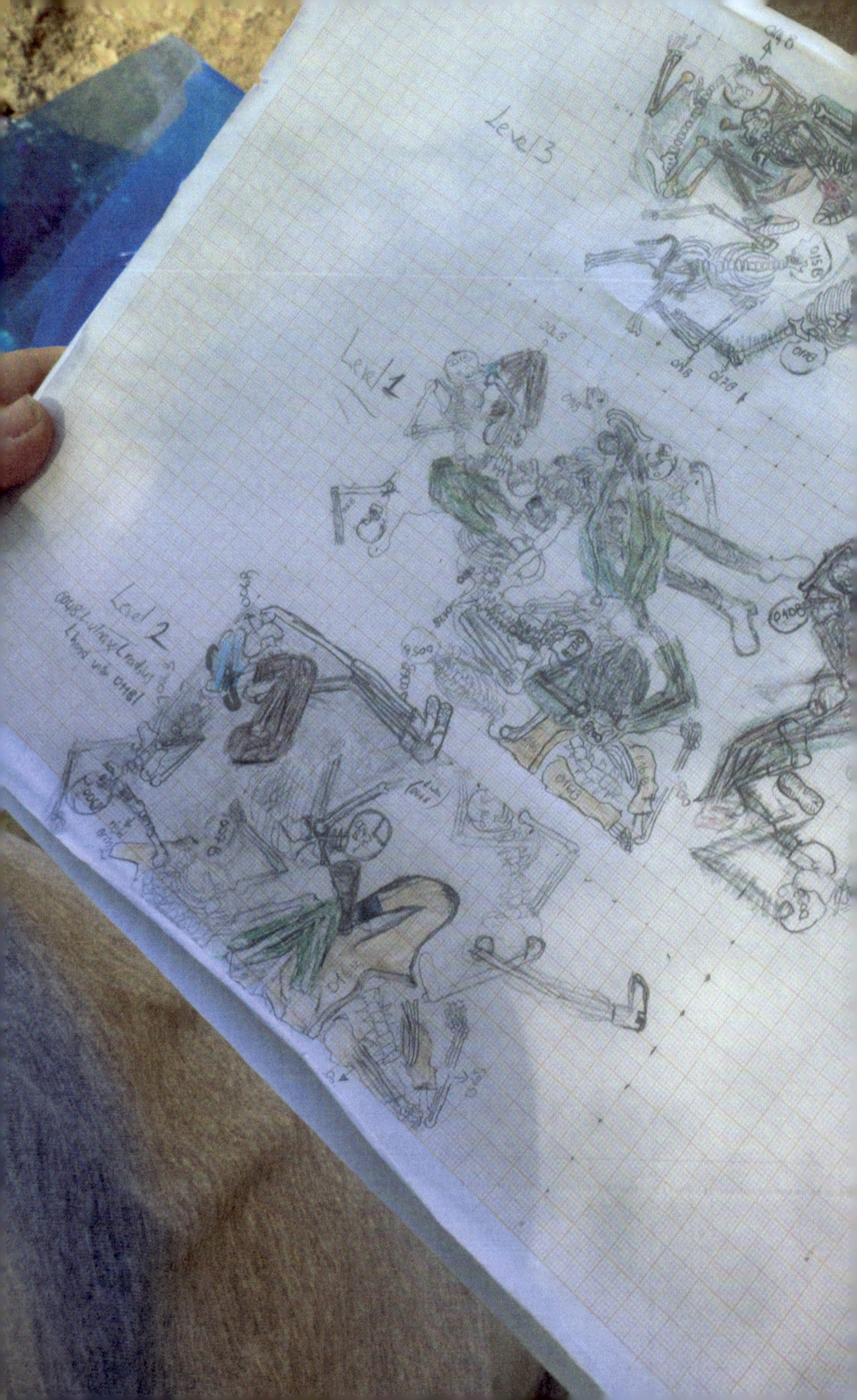
Level 3
Level 1
Level 2

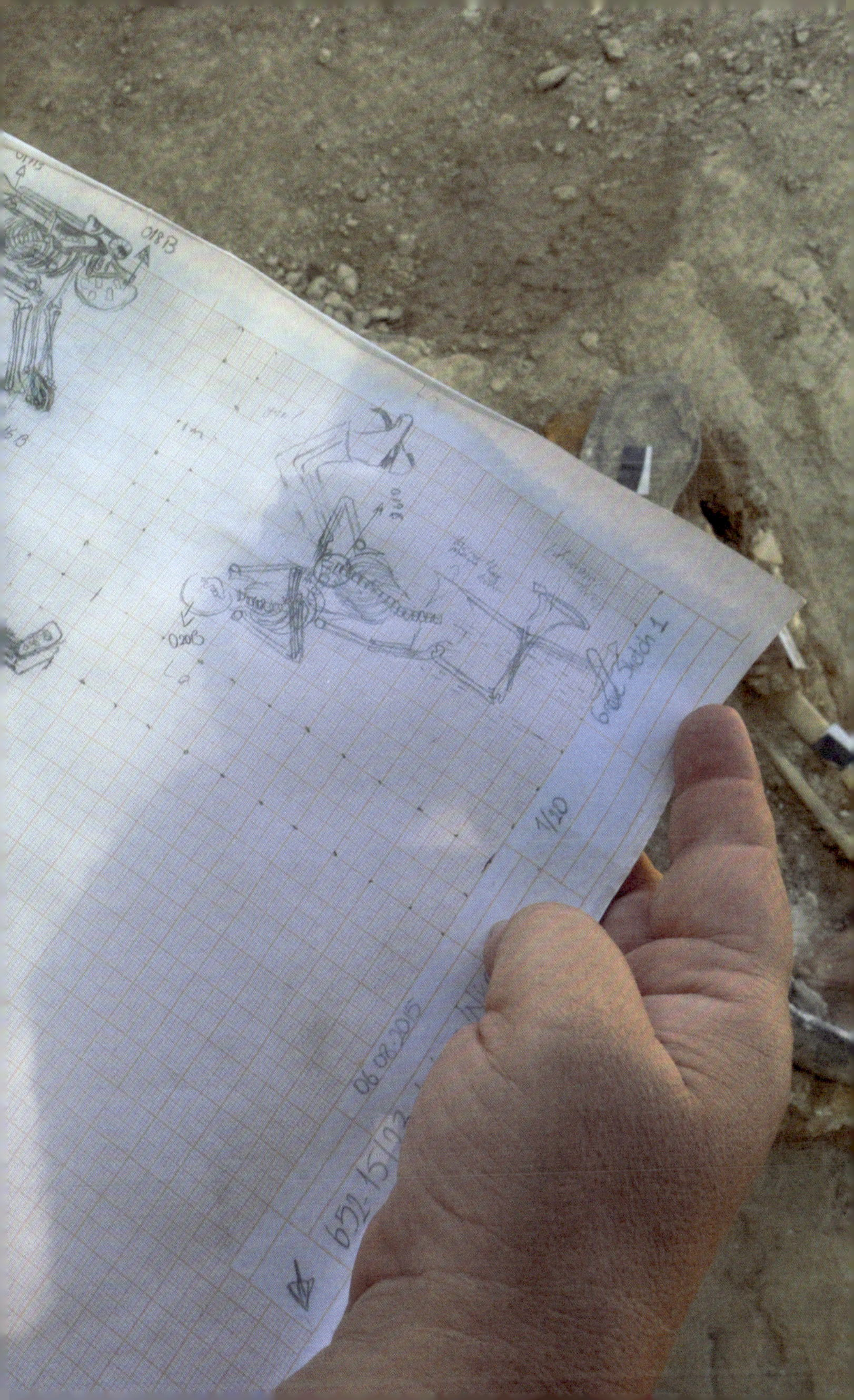
1/20
06.08.2015

'Coffee is like the glue between Cypriots,' said archaeologist Demet Karşılı. 'When we are arguing, we'll agree to stop for coffee, enjoy a chat and then – when the coffee is finished – continue with the argument.'

Demet Karşılı

In antiquity Cyprus lay on one of the busiest shipping routes in the Mediterranean. Phoenician galleys and Greek triremes sheltered in its bays en route to Antioch and Alexandria. Persian flotillas and Roman traders came ashore between Anatolia and the Levant. Arab pirates plundered and plucked slaves from the island's coastal villages, driving the Cypriots inland to safer hilltop hamlets. Crusader barques took refuge from storms on their way to the Holy Land. Later Venetian and Ottoman fleets – and then British frigates – dropped anchor in the waters where Europe merges with Asia. Over the millennia the islanders came to live in an interknit mosaic of villages: embracing and fighting the incomers, marrying and feuding with each other. Until the twentieth century. Then a 180-kilometre line was drawn across the island, from Famagusta in the east through the heart of Nicosia to the beautiful Bay of Morphou in the west.

'I grew up near Morphou,' said Demet Karşılı, 35, her eyes sparkling with happy childhood memories. 'When I was eight years old my mother woke me one winter morning and said, "I have a surprise for you." I jumped out of bed and ran to the balcony and saw snow on the peaks of the Troodos Mountains. Snow! The Troodos are the highest point on Cyprus and it's the only place on the island where it ever snows.'

'Let's go there now!' Demet had cried to her mother in excitement, and watched an unfamiliar look cross the woman's face.

'We can't,' said her mother.

'But why?'

'We just can't. Be happy that we live here in Morphou, near the sea.'

But Demet wasn't happy. Later that morning she and half-a-dozen equally excited neighbourhood children set out on a journey. When their parents' backs had been turned they snatched bread, tomatoes and halloumi and started to walk to the Troodos. But no more than 100 metres from home, their fathers caught them and ordered them to return home.

'But we want to go to the snow!' Demet had wailed as she was dragged through the orange groves back to the village.

Demet and her friends tried again both the next year and the year after that, not knowing that the 'Green Line' buffer zone divided their village from the mountains.

'I didn't touch snow until I was 23 years old,' Demet explained, pushing back her ponytail of gathered hair. 'The first winter after the border opened, I – like many Turkish Cypriots – drove south to the Troodos to see the snow, to throw snowballs. I met a Greek Cypriot there, and told him my story, and do you know what he told me? That he lived in a village in those mountains, and every summer from his balcony he had seen Morphou Bay, sparkling in the distance. Every summer he had pleaded with his mother to take him to the sea, and time and again she had refused him.'

Demet sighed and added, 'Our lives in Cyprus are so complicated. How can one ever explain it to a child?'

Home is central to a Cypriot's identity. When meeting a stranger, Cypriots will not first ask each other's name but rather 'Where are you from?' The question is posed to find connections, to establish links across generations, to place oneself by reaching into the past. 'Are you Mehmet's daughter? Is your father Yorgos of Agios Nikolaos? Do you know my uncle and your uncle once lived on the same street?'

Demet decided to become an archaeologist because she wanted to hear the voices of the past. In Famagusta she studied archaeology at the Eastern Mediterranean University and – despite the Republic of Cyprus's attempt to ban excavations in the north – helped to uncover a Neolithic site near to the village of Akanthou/Tatlısusite that could be the earliest settlement on the island.

'Prehistory fascinates me because there is no writing, no statues, only clues as to where people slept, where they ate. The archaeologist assembles the clues to understand – to hear the voices of – those people.'

Demet moved on to Ankara University and then to Ireland until she was approached to join the CMP, the first bi-communal project on Cyprus.

In the early days, the CMP employed only eight archaeologists: four Turkish Cypriots and four Greek Cypriots. All of them had worked previously on ancient sites. None of them knew how they would react to their first modern excavation. Demet did not have to wait long to find out. Two days into her first dig on the Mesaoria plain, she found the remains of a 14-year-old boy who had been killed in 1964.

'I was so nervous about touching the bones,' she recalled. 'The next day in the lab a colleague and I had to lay them out for the post-mortem. I remember that the boy's feet were still inside his socks, and that the socks were dark red,' she said, her voice shivering with emotion. 'I thought to myself, if this boy had lived he would be older than me now. I could have been his daughter, or even his granddaughter. Suddenly I couldn't take off his red socks. I couldn't take out the bones until my colleague saw my distress and whispered, "You must do it".' Demet paused, gathered herself and went on, 'And I did it, knowing that if I did not control my feelings I could not help the boy's family, I could not help Cyprus. I had to find a kind of inner peace, in the hope of finding a peace for Cyprus.'

Demet – a dynamic and vibrant young woman – has worked in the field for the CMP for almost a decade: helping to guide excavations, training newcomers, inspiring the whole team with her dedication and professionalism. In common with all of the scientists, she takes part in the final identification process as well as the return of the remains to the family. In a way, her work helps families to hear – and to be heard by – their loved one for the last time.

'Often I have to explain the archaeology to the family. But the first time I did it, I realised that they weren't listening to me. They weren't thinking about the depth at which the bones had been discovered or other technical details. They were just thinking about the lost years. So I said to them, as I now say to all the bereaved, "This has been an old wound that you have scratched and has festered for 50 years. Now at last it will close. Now there will be no more bleeding. Now it will slowly heal. But the scar will always remain.'

Demet took a deep breath and concluded, 'People talk about the Cyprus problem. I prefer to say the Cyprus solution. I believe together we are taking practical steps to work towards a solution.'

Some mornings archaeologist Christiana Zenonos wakes filled with sadness, knowing that she is likely to discover bones that day 'I'm good at my work. I like being outside. I'm adventurous. But my feelings are so mixed. I have a connection with all the people who suffered through the war.'

Christiana Zenonos

'He had been dropped into the well and left to die,' said Christiana Zenonos. 'A colleague who'd just returned from maternity leave heard him first. She thought that she was imagining her own baby. But then we all heard his cries, at the bottom of the shaft.'

Under the baking summer sun Christiana and her team had been excavating an old well for over a week. First a wheeled loader had sliced a steep ramp deep into the rocky earth. Then a tracked excavator had dug down to the bottom of the well. Christiana and her team had sifted through every scoop of earth, breaking apart clumps of muddy soil in their search for the remains of four men rumoured to have been dropped into the well 40 years earlier. They had never expected to hear living, plaintive cries.

'Suddenly we saw him at the very bottom of the well,' she said, her brown eyes damp with emotion. 'Another colleague climbed down, picked him up and gave him to me. He was so small that he fitted into the palm of my hand. We ran to the village to get milk and food. I called him Memo, which is a Turkish name.'

That evening Christiana carried the kitten across the Green Line hidden in a shopping bag. At home she made a bed for him out of her work shirt.

'He was like a gift for me,' she said.

No human remains were found in the well.

When she was 19 years old, Christiana's mother Maria had been driven from her home. For centuries the island's two communities had lived together in relative harmony: on whitewashed village squares, in cafés next to church or mosque, in abutting fields. Then suddenly they lived together in fear. In 1974 Christiana's mother Maria had been locked in a makeshift storehouse prison with all the Greeks in their north Cyprus village. Her father, a landowner, had been taken away. When the villagers had been released they'd fled south to Nicosia, without him.

'My grandmother cried for years,' recalled Christiana. 'She wrote poems about her lost husband and lost village. She was so angry that if, as a child, I switched on the television to watch Turkish cartoons, she would yell at me to turn it off.'

An unspoken sadness hung in the air despite her warm brown eyes and easy personality.

'But I wasn't angry. I was curious. I dreamed of becoming a journalist and meeting the leader of the Turkish Cypriots. I wanted to ask him why it had happened? Why we couldn't live together?'

In 2003 when the border opened her family drove north to her mother's old village. To reach it they followed her precise directions, until they reached the outskirts of the village. Suddenly Christiana's mother lost her way.

'I don't remember any more,' she said, overwhelmed by her feelings.

Nevertheless the family found the house and its new occupiers who invited them indoors, offering them coffee.

'Of course we did not want their coffee,' recalled Christiana. 'It was not a nice day.'

Christiana's mother would never again return to the northern part of the island. Yet Christiana herself remained curious. When the island's authorities released an official list of the names of the missing (including her grandfather), she began to plot their home villages on a map.

'I wanted to discover things for myself. I didn't understand why other people weren't curious,' she said with a smile, brushing back her hair. 'But it was also a kind of therapy. In Greek we have an expression *Yia tin psihi tis manas mou*, which means "I am doing this for my mother's soul". You know that *manas mou* can mean both my mother and my country.'

In 2009 Christiana applied for an archaeological post at the CMP. 'For me Cyprus is something that has been broken into very small pieces and needs to be slowly, carefully put back together. With the CMP I feel that we are helping to reassemble the island. I don't know if this can be done in a political context but I do know that the families can be helped. Our work is a way of showing that there is a good side to people.'

Yet her grandfather Kypros – a name that means Cyprus – remains among the missing.

'A few years ago a Turkish Cypriot man from my mother's village came looking for my family,' she said. 'He had cancer and – so as to be relieved from the burden – he wanted to tell us where my grandfather's body had been buried. But when my CMP colleagues went to the spot, the new landowner refused to give them access, which is very unusual. He even fenced off the area.'

Christiana sighed, in acceptance perhaps of the crimes and injustices that still haunt this island.

Christiana, now aged 33, has not counted how many individuals' remains she has recovered from the earth over the years. But at every site she has worked she has pocketed a single, small stone. Today they are gathered together in her Nicosia apartment as silent witnesses both to lives lost and to life ongoing.

'As well as the stones and Memo, I have a dog,' she said while stroking the lazy, lounging cat on her lap. 'Once when we were trenching a field in Famagusta, I came across six newborn puppies. They were starving and the weakest one was being pushed away by its siblings. I shared my tuna salad lunch with him and, at the end of the day, I realised that I couldn't leave him behind. I made a collar and lead out of security tape and took him home. I named him Phivos which means light in ancient Greek.'

Christiana nodded at Phivos, dozing at her feet then added, 'He is a real Cyprus dog, a mix.'

'When the work is finished here on Cyprus, I may travel to other former war zones,' said Christiana while playing with her dog Phivos. 'So now when I have an argument with my boyfriend, or when he's not nice to me, I tell him I want to go to Iraq.'

Mehmet Zorba, 34, is a CMP digger and vehicle operator. His great grandfather owned one of the camel trains that once crisscrossed the island. In 1963 his grandfather – who was also a driver – went missing on a journey home from work. Forty-five years later Mehmet operated the digger that uncovered his remains.

Mehmet Zorba

On the slender Karpas peninsula, goats and sheep cluster in the shade of blackened olive trees. Scorching wind and waves roll off the eastern Mediterranean. Broom and pines stir on the parched flanks of the Kyrenia Mountains. Wild donkeys wander about, oblivious to the ferocious heat. The ancients likened the shape of Cyprus to a deerskin spread on the sea, with its long tail of the Karpas tapering away to the east. On its Kral Tepesi or King's Mountain – which rises high above Kaleburnu – wealthy merchants once buried bronze sickles, incense burners, crystal stoppers for perfume bottles and ceramic stirrup jars, in the richest Bronze Age hoard ever discovered in Cyprus. Near to the village, Byzantine landlords raised jewel-like churches, the Templars erected castles and in 1572 an Ottoman pasha built a mosque beside the Ayia Annana monastery. Yet for all the rich and complex history, it is a place resonant with ruin.

At the start of the twentieth century Mehmet Zorba's great-grandfather was a camel owner, running his animal train west from the Karpas to Famagusta, Boghazi and even Nicosia. Thirty years later Mehmet's grandfather, Ali Zorba, sold the family's last 13 camels to buy a truck, one of the first to reach Kaleburnu. He was determined to carry forward his family's transport business on four wheels rather than four legs. Yet fortune did not smile on

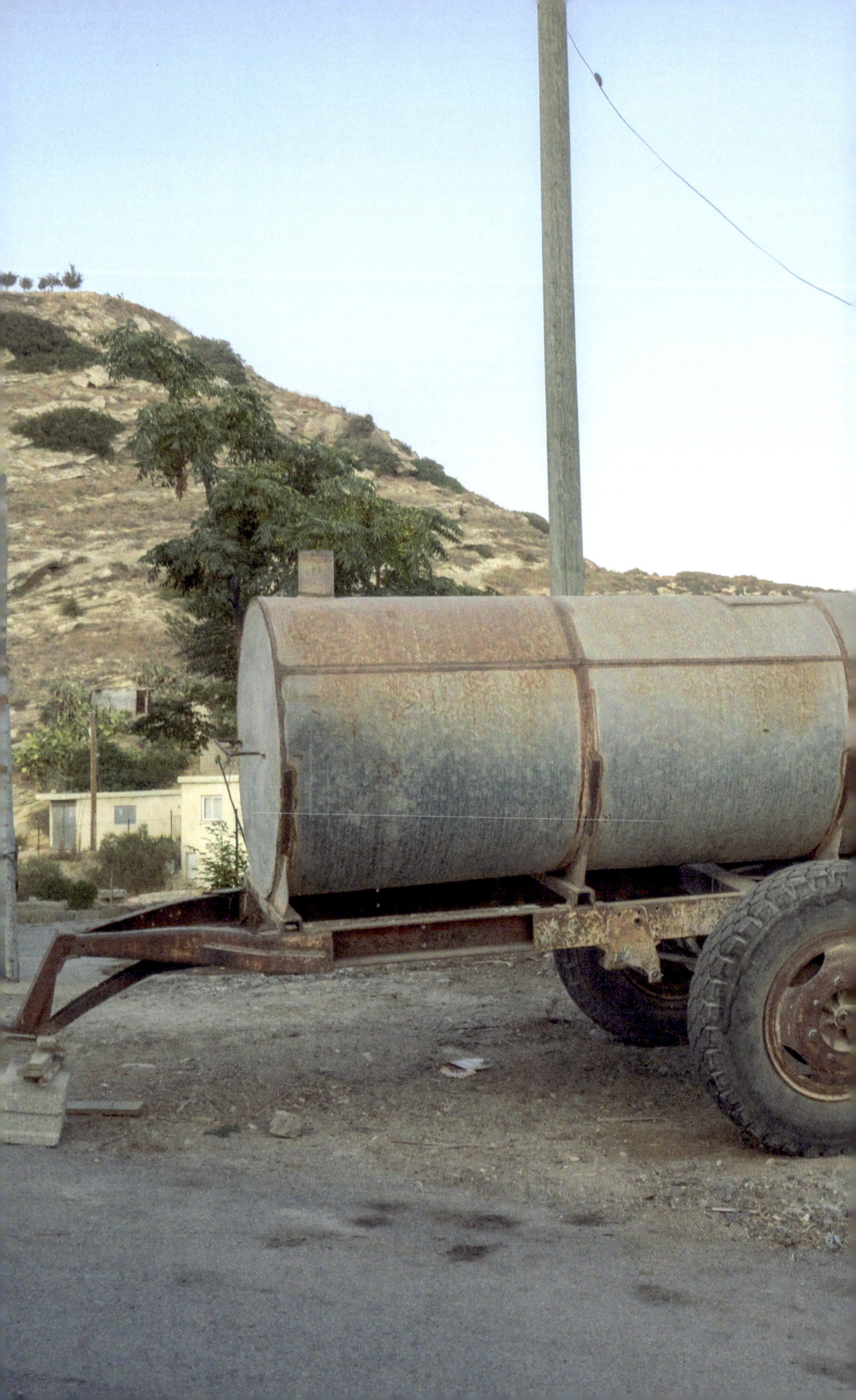

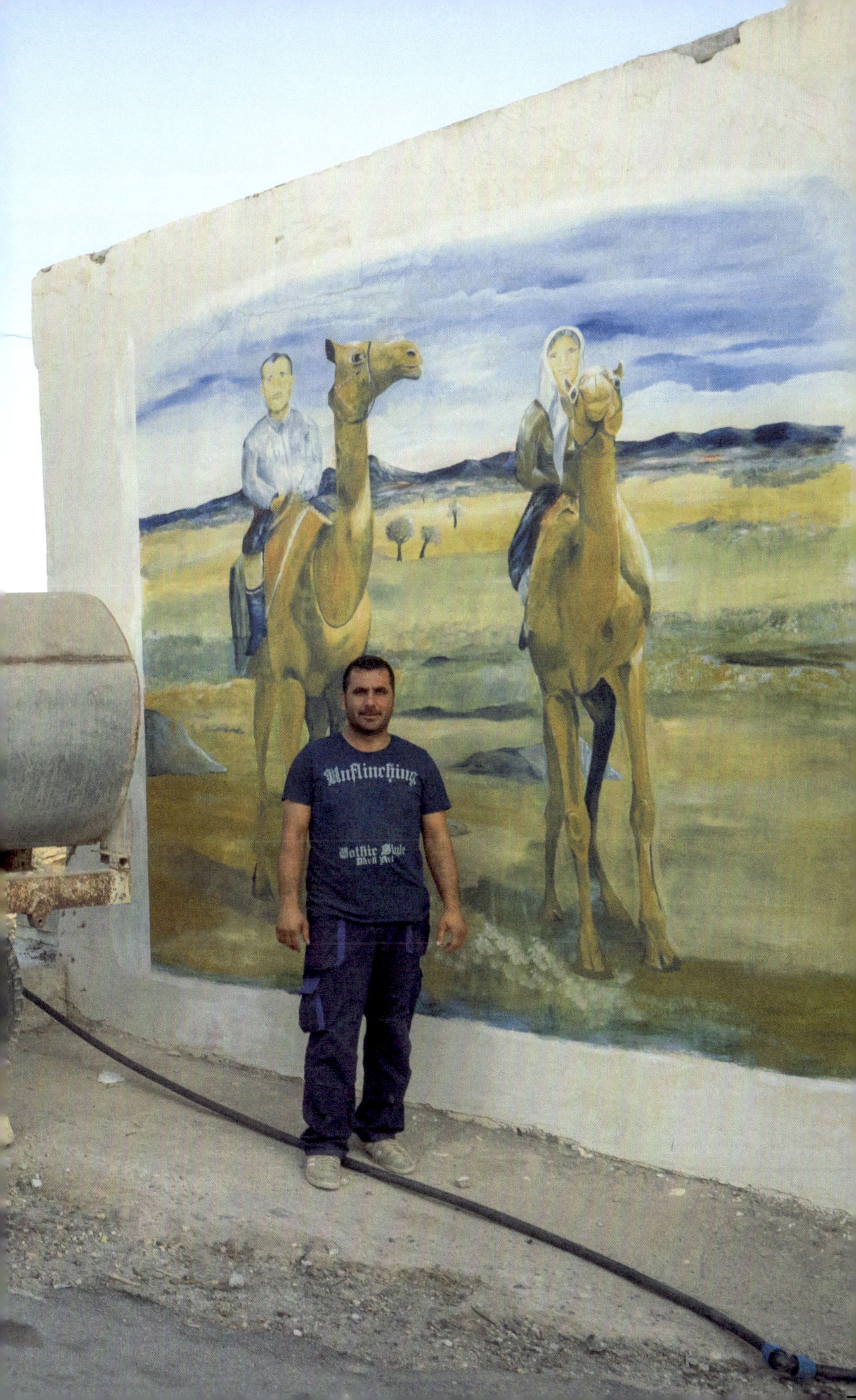
Unflinching
Gothic Style

the family, or on the village. Its wells dried up, its young people moved away and two of its finest men were killed on a tragic Friday night.

In 1963 Ali Zorba set off from Famagusta on the 60-kilometre drive for home. His cousin rode beside him in the passenger seat. Somewhere along the dark Karpas road, Ali, his cousin and the truck vanished.

After the disappearance, Ali's widow – Mehmet's grandmother – struggled to survive. She was only 32, a mother of five children, the youngest of whom was just 15 days old. She found work in the fields harvesting corn and tobacco, and shepherding neighbours' flocks. Later she served as a hotel chambermaid. Yet some days her children ate nothing more than two slices of bread. Hence as soon as he was old enough, her eldest son – Mehmet's father – learnt to drive. He joined the army and trained as a welder. After his release he earned enough money to buy a second-hand truck and then a JCB: transporting goods, digging foundations and fetching sand and shingle from the shore to use as building material in Kaleburnu.

In turn his son Mehmet also became a driver.

'He was my calmest child,' said Mousa, Mehmet's father. 'He needed no toys because he played with real tractors and diggers.'

In 2008 an anonymous informant revealed where Mehmet's grandfather had been buried 45 years earlier. The CMP hired Mehmet's father's digger, and asked him to operate it. Dozens of villagers gathered at the site on the Famagusta–Kaleburnu road, pushing forward in their hope to be the first to spot the remains. But as the days passed their anticipation dissipated. The informants were asked for more specific information, and the search was refined, yet still nothing was found. Mehmet's father began to lose hope, and one day after lunch he asked Mehmet to take over.

'I didn't have the heart to work any longer,' recalled Mousa.

Within minutes Mehmet's scoop unearthed a thighbone.

'I knew right away that it was my grandfather,' said Mehmet.

The CMP archaeologists then secured the site and proceeded to exhume the remains. DNA testing would take another month, confirming the link between grandfather and father as well as the identity of the cousin's skeleton, but the family needed no scientific proof.

'Did you find him today?' Mehmet's grandmother asked him when he came home that evening.

'Yes,' Mehmet answered, and described to her the shirt, trousers and shoes that had been found in the rough grave.

'Those were his clothes. That is him,' she replied.

Today minarets and pylons advance over the mountain ridge along the Karpas. On the valley floor new plastic pipes – fed by the world's longest undersea water pipeline – bring drinking and irrigation water from Turkey. Mehmet – who joined the CMP after the discovery of his grandfather's remains – sits with his parents on their shady balcony in their house on the flank of King's Mountain, not far from where the Bronze Age hoard was discovered. They talk of better days returning to Kaleburnu, of new roads and beach hotels rising along the peninsula's southern shore.

With them sits an older relative who had known Mehmet's grandfather Ali. He shakes his head with incomprehension, almost half a century after the murder.

'Ali Zorba was a likeable, harmless person. He got on with everyone,' he says. 'Why on earth would anyone want to kill him?'

Mehmet Zorba, right, sits with his father Mousa and mother Hayriye on their balcony on the Karpas peninsula. Most often instead of missing Cypriots, the archaeologists and their support staff find only rocks at excavations.

Archaeologist Maria Solomou prepares a numbered ID card prior to photographing a newly-discovered grave. Every set of remains or body parts is given a unique identifying number to ensure both the individuality and the anonymity of the missing person through all stages of scientific process.

Maria Solomou

No day passes without Maria Solomou's father mentioning the house that he left behind in the north. Time and again he describes its walls and rooms. He ruminates on its garden, shares his photographs of its fig and almond trees. He recalls the arrival in 1965 of the first telephone, which when it rang any passing soul might pick up and shout across the fields for the person wanted by the caller. He reminisces about harvesting beans and watermelon, about Agios Ermolaos' two rivers that hardly ever ran dry, about his work as the village jeweller. Finally he tells Maria Solomou where the first shells exploded in 1974.

In 1974 – following the arrival of the Turkish Army – the once-mixed village had been emptied of its people. A year or two later displaced Turkish Cypriots began to move into the abandoned houses. In 2003 when the border opened for the first time in three decades, Maria Solomou's father took her to Agios Ermolaos, 18 kilometres northwest of Nicosia on the southern slopes of the Kyrenia mountain range. In the tiny square he asked her to point to his house. She did not hesitate, even though she had never before visited the village.

'"It's down there on the left, Papa," I said,' recalled Maria Solomou, silver rings flashing on her muscular hands. 'I knew it right away.'

At the time the house was still unoccupied and father and daughter picked their way with care around its precarious walls and memories. They spoke in whispers as if not to disturb the past. They did not enter the padlocked building.

After university, Maria Solomou – a tall and slender 35-year-old who had trained as an archaeologist – joined the Department of Antiquities and later on the police force.

'I thought that I should have a safe, government job,' she said with a laugh. 'But you know, I couldn't stand working in an office or being told to polish my shoes or to change my hair. I wanted to be outside in the sun.'

She seized the chance to work for the CMP, travelling every day over the Buffer Zone and into the north. In the Mediterranean heat a buried body decays away in only three months, but its bones can last for centuries. Hence during their excavations, Maria Solomou and her colleagues often find medieval, Roman and even Hellenistic bones, as well as those of the missing.

'It's exciting when we find remains yet the discovery also leaves us feeling so sad,' she admitted.

Then one day Maria Solomou was asked to excavate a site in her father's old village.

'Over the years I'd kept an eye on the old family house. So when we started in Agios Ermolaos, I noticed right away that someone had moved into it. That evening I told my father and the next day I tried to visit,' said Maria. 'But the new owner refused to let me cross the threshold. It broke my heart.'

Nevertheless Maria Solomou's father – whose name is Konstantinos – began to come back to the village: to walk along its lanes, to remember the site of the bakery and the cobbler, to retrace the trails into the mountains where once he had collected mushrooms and hunted white doves.

'In part he is reliving his childhood of course,' admitted Maria Solomou, 'but he is also thinking of how different his life might have been if…'.

Today Konstantinos, 65, plans to publish a collection of photographs of his old village. To write it he has unpicked the village's complex history, from being almost wholly Muslim in the nineteenth century to having a Christian majority one hundred years later. In 1964 its last Turkish Cypriots had fled to take refuge in nearby hamlets. Ten years later its Greek Cypriots – including Konstantinos – had themselves fled ahead of the advancing Turkish army. After that the original Turkish Cypriots were relocated back to the village, along with other families displaced from the south. Over time the village's name has also changed. To Greek Cypriots it will always be Agios Ermolaos. To the original Turkish Cypriot residents it is Ayirmola.

Every month or two Konstantinos still travels over the Green Line from Nicosia to sit in the old café under the vines, to talk about his photo album and to share his collection of 500 photographs with local men. His best friend in the village is also a refugee, a Turkish Cypriot who had been moved in the opposite direction in 1974 from Paphos in the south to Agios Ermolaos/ Ayirmola in the north. Together they share a longing for a lost, romanticised past. In the café nobody talks of the future.

At the same time, at the bottom of the hill beyond the abandoned and unattended churchyard, Maria Solomou and her team are excavating yet another field. In 1974 four young villagers – all friends of Konstantinos – went missing from the village. More than 40 years on, an unnamed local told CMP investigators where their remains might be found.

'I lost no one in my family, thank God, but there are many who have been waiting 40 or 50 years for news of their loved ones,' Maria Solomou said. 'Even if they know that their father or brother must be dead, they need to have a funeral, to have a place to pray for their soul. It's vital for them, and it is for them that I work.'

A sudden rush of goose bumps then betrayed her high emotion.

'But to do it here, in the fields where my father played when he was a boy, it is so moving for me. Even though I never lived in this village, I feel like I am a part of it. I feel that I belong here.'

Maria Solomou's father Konstantinos, left, visits his old village and sits with his friend Özel. Once the cousin of one of Maria's colleagues claimed that he could tell a Greek Cypriot from a Turkish Cypriot just by looking at their face. So Maria's colleague decided to test him on it, and showed him photographs of all the CMP team members who come from both communities. 'And do you know what? He was 100% wrong,' said Maria's colleague.

In common with all his young colleagues, Evren Korkmaz joined the CMP team filled with enthusiasm and determination. In the process of exhuming and examining the bones, both archaeologists and anthropologists often come to feel that they know the missing person.

Evren Korkmaz

'This is my village and my home,' said Evren Korkmaz, 33, spreading his arms as if to embrace all Rizokarpaso/Dipkarpaz, the most easterly town on the island. 'Of course this house once belonged to a Greek. But I grew up here. I smoked my first cigarette here. I had my first and my best friends here. And I learnt to play cards here.'

In 1974 Evren's father Hasan had come to the island under a parachute. He was a karasakal – or 'black beard' – as the Turkish soldiers were then nicknamed, men who had been unable to shave during the weeks of fighting. In common with incomers throughout history, Hasan had liked the island and decided to stay, joining the police force and convincing both his father and mother to follow him to Cyprus. Together they settled in Rizokarpaso/Dipkarpaz, where Hasan married a local girl who gave him two children, one of whom was Evren.

'I am Cypriot even though my father came from Turkey,' said Evren.

After 1974 some 2,500 Greek Cypriots had left the town. Some Turkish Cypriots moved in to the area but for the most part incomers from Anatolia repopulated the vacated houses. Today about one third of the population of the north have Turkish citizenship. Rizokarpaso/Dipkarpaz and Agias Trias/Sipahi are the only villages in the north with a few hundred remaining Greek Cypriots (about 10% of the village population in 2016).

'But there are no jobs here for anyone,' said Evren. 'Young people who stay here can only find work in farming or with the local council.'

Evren decided to become an archaeologist because no one else in the village had ever done such work and because 'we have many ancient sites in Cyprus'. But university came as a shock to him because he knew no one.

'Here everyone knows me and I know everyone.'

After graduation from Cyprus Eastern Mediterranean University, Evren completed his military service and then joined the CMP, settling in Famagusta. Although he came home less and less often (in part because 'there is no one to play cards with anymore'), Rizokarpaso/Dipkarpaz remained his home. As in much of the region, village ties are often stronger than any other links.

Evren's father Hasan also moved on, leaving both his wife and the police force to open a simple tourist hotel at the tip of the Karpas peninsula. On a pristine beach in the wildest and most unspoilt part of the island, he built a series of wooden bungalows, adding a new building or two every year.

'When I was a policeman, I used to drive out here and dream of living by the sea. Now my life is like a dream come true,' said Hasan in broken English.

Behind them Russian, German and Swedish holidaymakers

laughed in a rustic, bamboo canopy shelter.

'I am proud of my son. He has a good job, and the work that he does is good for Cyprus,' Hasan went on. 'No war is good and so many people are now gone. But Evren helps a son or a grandchild to know what happened to their grandfather or their father. This is important.'

Archaeologist Andria Avgousti, centre, works with her colleagues at a new gravesite. Farmers are compensated for excavations on their land.

Andria Avgousti

'Out! Get out!' shouted Andria Avgousti, 28.

She and her colleagues ran up the steep ramp, fearful that an explosion would bring the high, rough earthen walls crashing down on them. Shrapnel could shower them and the noise panic children who were congregating at the nearby K-Cineplex. Andria ran for her life, expecting at any moment for it to end.

Over the previous eight months the CMP had dug deep into the earth to access the bottom of two old wells. That morning Andria and her team had been at the foot of the ramp, examining the soil clawed out by a tracked excavator. Broken tools, tyres, rusted farming implements and sheep bones came to light. Then a pink plastic bag landed at the archaeologists' feet. The young women began to pick it apart with their hoes. Inside, wrapped in newspaper, were two live grenades.

At the top of the ramp, as soon as they caught their breath, one of Andria's colleagues called the police. Within minutes the bomb disposal unit arrived, secured the grenades in a metal box and drove them outside town to detonate them safely.

In years past Strovolos had been a farmland of citrus orchards and open fields on the outskirts of Nicosia. Andria's grandfather had moved to the area to find agricultural work, leaving his pregnant wife in her home village in Pitsilia. But as sporadic fighting spread across the island, Andria's grandmother had loaded her children, her goat and herself onto a bus and followed her husband to Strovolos, and out of danger. But then one night they were awoken by shouts and gunfire. In the morning there was no evidence of any disturbance, except for a discarded shoe near to the head of one of the local wells. Soon afterwards Andria's grandparents had moved again, into Nicosia.

An unknown number of Turkish Cypriots were said to have been thrown down the orchards' wells during the 1963 crisis. But by 2015 Strovolos had grown into the second largest municipality in Cyprus, home to 70,000 people spread across six parishes. Their houses, shops, supermarkets and the K-Cineplex cinema now surrounded the suspected wells.

As she'd lost no members of her family, Andria grew up without the emotional burden that weighs on most Cypriots. She was less susceptible to haunting tales of one community's victimhood, and the other's cruelty and injustice. Yet at school she was never taught that Greek Cypriots had killed Turkish Cypriots. When she was offered work with the CMP, she saw it as a once-in-a-lifetime opportunity to discover the truth about Cyprus.

'I became an archaeologist because of my love of mythology. I studied at Thessaloniki and at the Ecole du Louvre in Paris,' she said. 'But I came home because I needed to feel my roots. At the age of 25 I had only once crossed the Green Line. I realised how very much I wanted to see the other side, even to learn to speak

Turkish. And do you know what surprised me when I went to the north? That it was so similar: the same people, the same architecture, the same gardens, the same tastes and smells. I realised how alike we are, and how most of us do not want to see it.'

In her work at the CMP, Andria – like many of her young colleagues – believed that she was 'participating in history'.

'In the beginning we believed that we were the new generation, and that feeling filled us with hope.'

But as time passed, Andria began to lose her hope for new beginnings.

'I realised that until we stop teaching bad history, until the schoolbooks are changed, nothing will change on the island.'

In many schools in the south, exercise books are printed with an emotive photograph of Kyrenia harbour – now under Turkish Cypriot administration – and the words, 'I will not forget'.

'In my opinion no political party has presented any real solutions because we – the Cypriots – don't really know what we want to become. So what happens if there is no solution? Young people will continue to lose interest in the other side. They will think more and more about their jobs or their car and their new iPhone. In time the Cyprus problem will become insoluble.'

After the departure of the bomb disposal unit, work resumed on the Strovolos site but – in the end, after eight months' labour – no human remains were found at the bottom of either well.

'When an excavation isn't successful, I can feel cheated,' said Andria. 'We believed the informant. We worked for months under the sun and in the rain. Yet often in the end we find nothing.'

Three years on, Andria is excavating new sites at a dried lake outside Galateia/Mehmetçik. Some 60 Cypriots are believed to have been murdered here, their bodies dumped in shallow graves around the old lakeshore.

'Usually some villagers speak to us but never about our work or the past,' said Andria with resignation. 'Only after we had been here for a few weeks did one local man sidle up to a colleague and whisper to him, "Come with me. The bones are over there. You didn't see me. I didn't see you." Since then we have found the remains of three missing individuals.'

Yet despite the discoveries, Andria – a young, educated and open-minded young woman who speaks three languages – often feels cheated in her Cyprus.

Avgousti, right, celebrates her 28th birthday with friends in Nicosia. The CMP's bi-communal work is carried out by a new generation of Cypriots determined to heal the wounds left open by their fathers and grandfathers.

Anthropological Phase

At the CMP Anthropological Laboratory, twelve forensic anthropologists analyse exhumed remains. Working together in two bi-communal teams they assemble and associate individual bones with larger skeletal remains. Together they determine the sex and approximate age of the individual, look for identifying features such as pathologies or dental characteristics, and examine and record all clothing and personal belongings found among the remains. Small bone samples are then taken and sent abroad for DNA analysis.

The CMP Anthropological Laboratory is located in the United Nations Protected Area (UNPA) near the old Nicosia Airport. In addition to its fully equipped labs, this location also houses the Family Viewing Facility where the families of missing persons have the opportunity to meet with the scientists involved in the identification process and view the remains of their loved ones. Here the bereaved suffer their second trauma, facing the harsh reality and taking the necessary step to final closure.

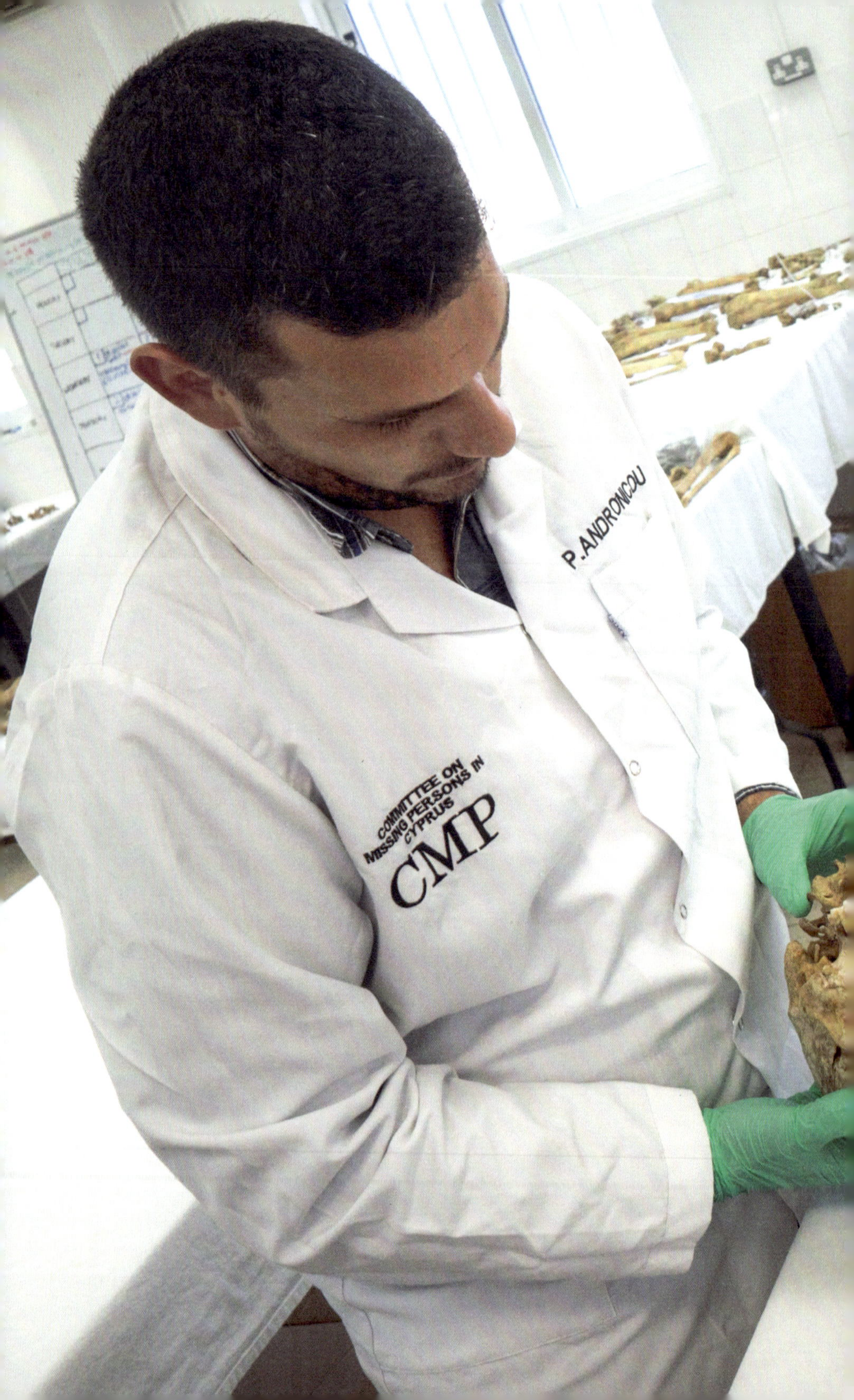
P.ANDRONICOU
COMMITTEE ON MISSING PERSONS IN CYPRUS
CMP

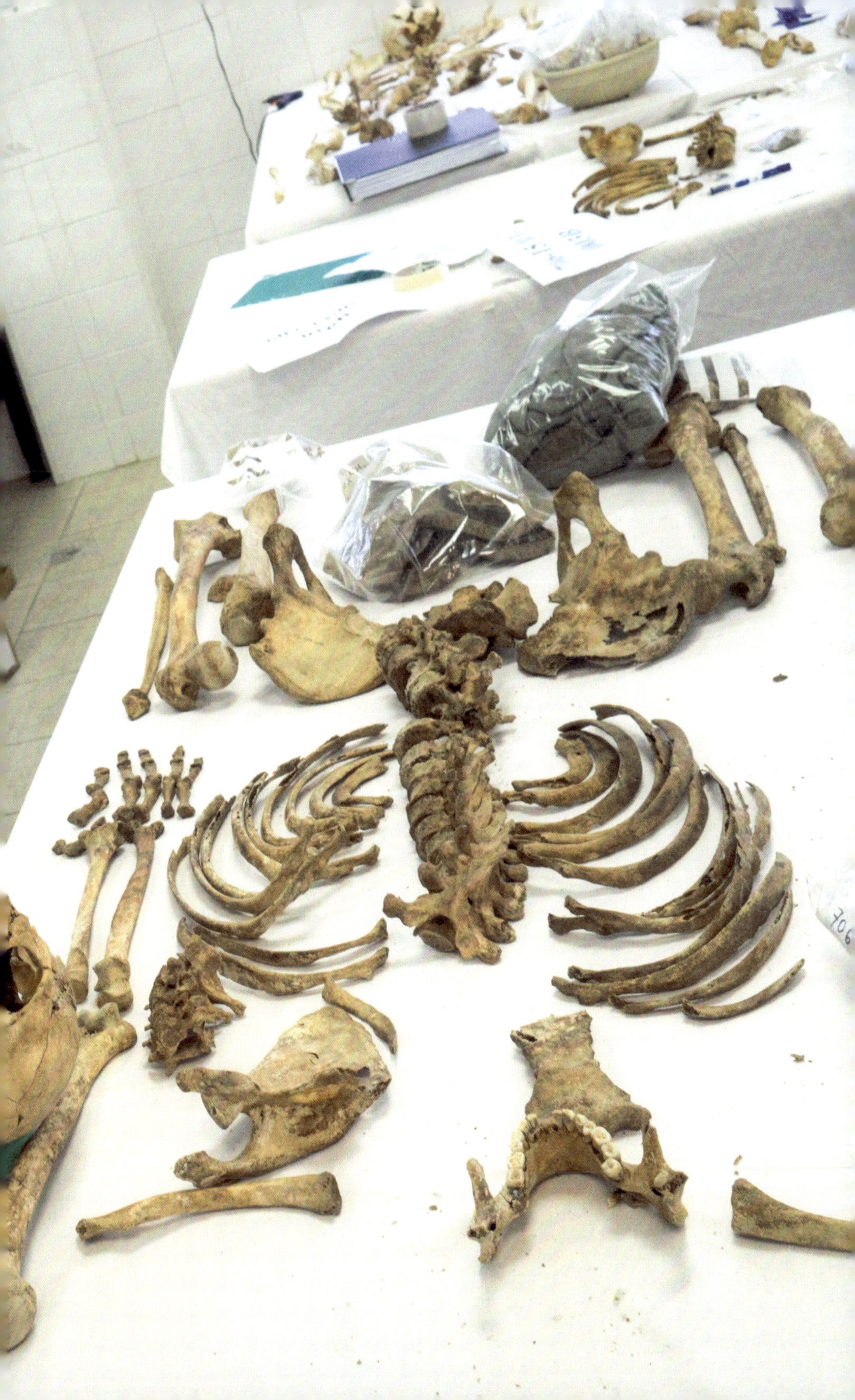

In the CMP Anthropological Laboratory, anthropologist Theodora Eleftheriou pieces together individual bones to establish the age, sex and height of a missing person.

Theodora Eleftheriou

As a child Theodora had loved her mother's fairy tales. At bedtime she had heard that rain was the tears of angels crying in heaven, that the wind soughing through the cypresses was the sound of the trees gossiping with each other. When Theodora started school, she also believed the stories that she was told. Only as an adult did she learn the difference between myth and reality in Cyprus.

'I've always been curious,' said Theodora, now 35. 'As a kid, I rode my bike all over our neighbourhood, collecting insects and flowers. I've always liked finding things, and mysteries, so I decided to study history and archaeology.'

Her curiosity led her from Thessaloniki to Sheffield University. 'I realised there that I was less interested in the monuments than the people behind them. I wanted to know the human story.'

On her graduation in 2005 Theodora returned to Cyprus, one of only two anthropologists in the south at the time. She became one of the CMP's first employees and found herself working alongside anthropologists and archaeologists from the north. She had never before met a Turkish Cypriot.

'Our first excavation was just outside Nicosia. We'd heard that a couple – a Turkish Cypriot couple – had been killed and buried.'

Ashamed by her partial knowledge of the recent history of Cyprus, Theodora threw herself into studying the island's past.

She wanted to understand its story from both points of view. Her daily interaction with colleagues – and the emotion behind their work – helped to forge strong bonds. Friendships began to bridge the divide.

'At first we couldn't talk about our work to anyone, even with our family, even when I came home with filthy clothes!'

In the early days it was feared that the CMP's work could be jeopardised if malicious rumours were spread before the first remains had been returned to families. But the early successes allayed those fears, by sparking a rush of popular support.

'For me it's hardest to deal with the missing children,' Theodora said. 'Once we were looking in a cemetery for a six-year-old Greek Cypriot child. There were rumours that the girl had been crying and – to shut her up – a soldier had cut her throat. We all hoped the rumour was untrue but we found a child's skeleton without a cranium. We were devastated. Months later the DNA results came back negative. We went back and searched again, and found the right skeleton … with cranium attached. As sad as it was we were so relieved to put the terrible rumour to rest. The first skeleton was then identified as much older, from long before the troubles, and the cranium was missing because the burial had been disturbed.'

After six months' work in the field, Theodora graduated to the CMP Anthropological Laboratory. Every weekday Greek Cypriot scientists from the south and Turkish Cypriot scientists from the north travel into no-man's-land to work there together.

'For me, the CMP matters for two reasons. The first is emotional; everything must be done for the families to close this terrible chapter,' she said. 'The second reason is both historical and political. A way must be found to reconcile the two communities, and to deepen communication and understanding between them. The Cyprus problem can only be solved once we have solved the problem of the missing.'

Every evening Theodora tells bedtime stories to her four-year-old daughter: about angels washing their clothes in heaven, about baby elephants needing nightly baths, about their special island home.

'My daughter loves the stories but as she grows older I will teach her only the facts,' said Theodora. 'I will tell her that she must read to understand. She will have to search on her own if she wants to know the truth.'

Following pages:
The more complete a skeleton, the easier becomes analysis and identification. 'It is a human right never to lose one's identity even after death,' said Eleftheriou with feeling. 'I want people to know of the importance of this work.'

COMMITTEE ON MISSING PERSONS IN CYPRUS
CMP
CAL
ANTHROPOLOGICAL LABORATORY

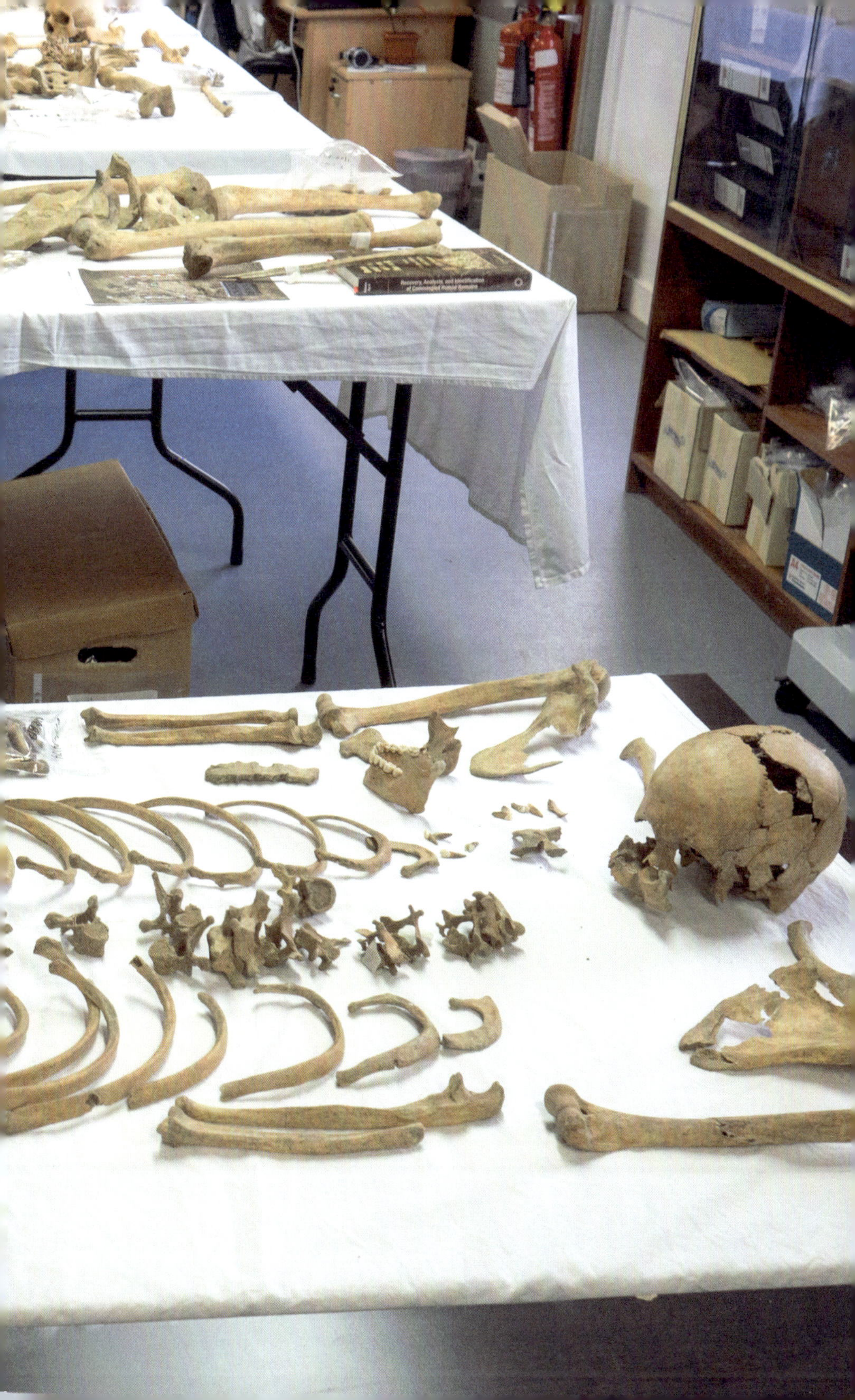

Anthropologist Uyum Vehit sits with his father Niyazi at the site of their old family home.

Uyum Vehit

'"How can you be friends with Greeks?" I once asked my father. "Don't you know what they did to us?"'

When he was a schoolboy, Uyum Vehit – in common with every child in the north of Cyprus – was taken to Nicosia's Museum of Barbarism, a shocking memorial that perpetrates the story of the brutal 1963 murder of a Turkish woman and her three children.

'The museum is arranged like a crime scene with blood on the walls,' said Uyum, shaking his head. 'After my school visit, I ran home and asked my father how he could ever be friends with Greeks.'

Uyum's school itself had been used to promote a similar narrative. It was named after a teacher who had been killed during the years of inter-communal violence. To this day the story of his murder is recounted in graphic detail on placards in the school foyer.

'In school we were taught that we Turkish Cypriots were the only victims. Now – through having made Greek Cypriot friends – I can see the other side of the coin. I realise that both sides suffered. My schooling was not full of lies but it was one-sided. It was education with a gap.'

Uyum, now 32, paused and said, 'In part I joined the CMP because it's about the only place on the island where people from the two communities can work together.'

'This was my village,' said Uyum's father Niyazi, a 70-year-old retired agricultural engineer, as he and Uyum picked their way across the dry, broken earth of vanished Agios Epifanios. Shattered roof tiles cracked under their feet. Beneath them spread the wide Solea valley, verdant with vines and clusters of olive, date and cypress trees.

In his youth Niyazi and his parents had grown peppers, artichokes and tomatoes on these high terraces. Niyazi had swum in the valley's swift Kariotis river, showered on its slopes gazing north toward distant mountains and a sliver of sea.

'It'd be impossible ever to find better tasting tomatoes,' he told Uyum with his voice full of emotion.

In the years since 1963, when Niyazi and 60 other villagers had been forced to flee, their homes had been looted, then torched and finally bulldozed into the dust. Even the local one-room Turkish schoolhouse and mosque had vanished

Niyazi stopped on a mound of rubble and said, 'This was my home.'

As a child growing up in the northern half of divided Nicosia, Uyum had dreamed of becoming an archaeologist.

'I was fascinated by what remained,' he said. 'My uncle had been an archaeologist and – when I was a young boy – he'd taken me to Salamis, the ancient Greek city-state on the east coast of Cyprus, to see and swim over the submerged ruins. It made a profound impression on me.'

But when the time came to choose a career, Uyum – perhaps because of his father Niyazi's displacement – announced that he planned to become a lawyer.

'But why law?' asked Niyazi.

'Because I need security and a regular salary,' he replied.

'Money and security will come later,' said Niyazi. 'Now you need to do what you love.'

So Uyum followed his heart, studying archaeology first in Cyprus and then at Edinburgh University. After graduation he worked in the UK for a private archaeological consultancy but in time he began to miss his family as well as the Mediterranean climate.

'I came home both for my country and for myself,' he said.

On his return Uyum volunteered to work for the CMP, moving from archaeology to anthropology in his desire to help to identify the island's missing people. Time and again over the years – in the field and at the lab – he has been moved beyond words by the realisation that this inter-communal work has helped to relieve the bereaved of their pain.

In recognition that the issue of the missing is a serious obstacle to peace, stability and reconciliation, Uyum has also contributed to the CMP's regional role. Cyprus lies less than 100 kilometres from the Syrian coast. In the region hundreds of thousands of people have gone missing through the years of wars and political repression. At the CMP, Uyum has taken part in the training of 25 Iraqi anthropologists and the visit of two forensic scientists from

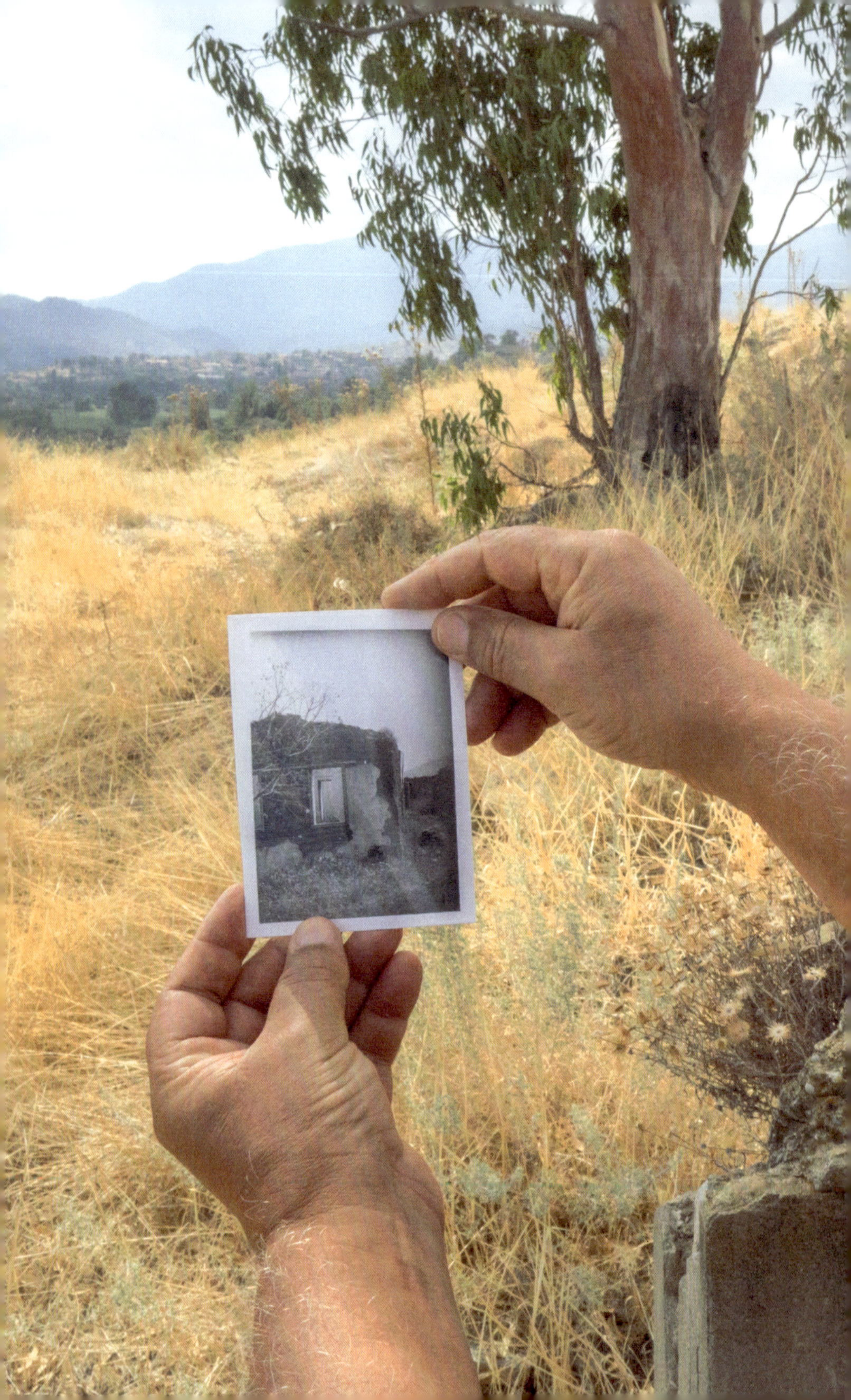

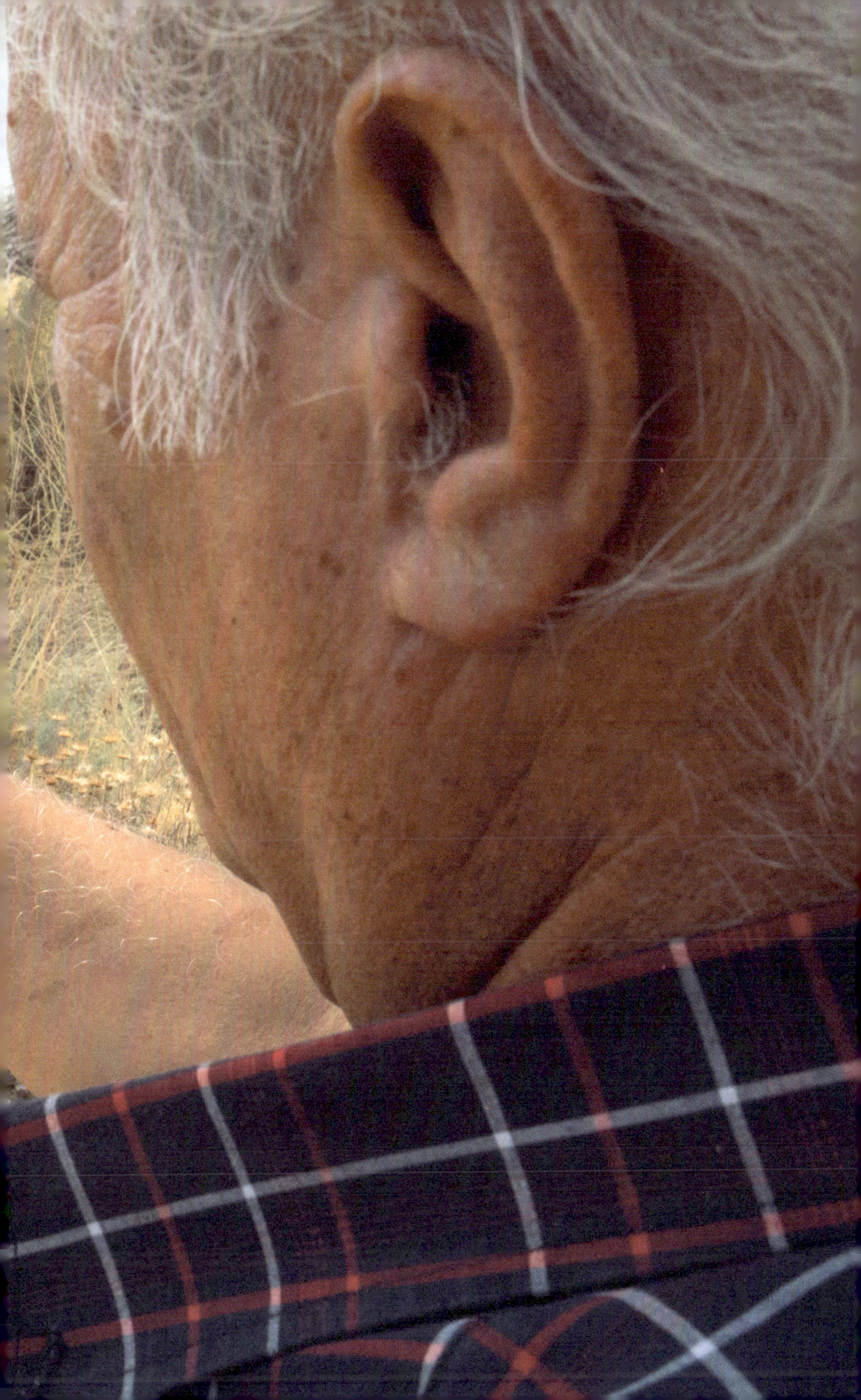

Lebanon. He has shared his expertise at pathology and trauma conferences in Turkey, Korea and the United States.

Uyum remembers his first visit to Agios Epifanios with his father.

'For almost 40 years my father had been unable to return home. Naturally he'd come to romanticise the life that had been left behind. He'd tell me that Agios Epifanios was set in Cyprus's most beautiful valley, that it grew the plumpest grapes and most tasty beans,' Uyum recalled. 'Over the years I'd heard so much about it that I had expected a kind of paradise. But when I came here with him it was... ordinary. Yet I realised how special it was in my father's eyes, and that moved me deeply.'

As father and son sat together on a rough cement water fountain, Niyazi suddenly started to laugh. 'And do you remember on that first visit the woman in the café?' he said.

Uyum shook his head.

'Over there across the valley we stopped for a coffee,' said Niyazi pointing to a nearby village. 'A Greek woman came up to me and said, "Are you Niyazi Vehit?" I didn't remember her but she – blushing like a young girl – said, "In the summertime you used to shower in the open air behind your house across the valley in Agios Epifanios. And I used to watch you."'

Niyazi and Uyum laughed together, thinking of lives that might have been. Together they stood to leave the valley and return to the north. A soaring eucalyptus tree planted by Niyazi's mother as a sapling rose behind the fountain. On the base of the fountain – built by the British in 1953 – another refugee had roughly painted his name as well as that of his lost village home. Like Niyazi, he had had to leave his home. He had been displaced from the north to the south not so many years after Niyazi had moved in the opposite direction.

Previous pages:
Niyazi Vehit holds a black-and-white picture of his old home, snapped shortly after the family was forced to abandon the building. It would be understandable if he had remained bitter yet today he feels no anger, and his courage and compassion have shaped his son Uyum's life.

The reconstruction of a foot or hand – made up respectively of 26 and 27 individual bones – is like a puzzle for anthropologist and osteologist Photis Andronicou. In common with his colleagues, he works on a dozen or more cases at once. In order to accelerate the pace of identification, the CMP has doubled the size of the laboratory since 2012.

Photis Andronicou

Within the ring of massive Venetian walls, old Nicosia is a maze of narrow lanes, Gothic arches and modern-day concrete hotels. Here in the twelfth century, Lusignan monarchs once ruled Europe's easternmost Christian kingdom. Here their king Peter I launched a crusade against Egypt. Here tens of thousands died when the city fell to the Ottomans. Here as a child, Photis Andronicou explored the labyrinthine capital.

On foot and by bicycle Photis ventured from his front door to the corner café and on to St John's Cathedral, where a finger of John the Baptist was said to have been preserved until stolen by Egyptian Mamelukes. As he grew older he went further afield, as far as his grandfather's suitcase factory and the Archbishop's Palace that Greek tanks had surrounded during the 1974 military coup d'état. At home his grandmother regaled him with stories of those days, of the burning palace and the Turkish response. In his vivid childish imagination Photis compressed and embellished the medieval and modern then excitedly repeated the tales to his father Vasos. In reply his father told him, 'My son, when you grow up you'll see things differently.'

Photis became fascinated by biology and then forensic science long before the popularity of the American television series *CSI: Crime Scene Investigation*. At Nottingham Trent University and then University College London, he specialised in forensic anthropology.

'After completing my Masters, my plan was to stay in the UK to do a PhD or to join Scotland Yard,' said the now 30-year-old Photis. 'Then a cousin rang to tell me about the CMP. Right away I came home, and I haven't looked back.'

At the Anthropological Laboratory, in his white coat, Photis explained the process of the analysis and identification of remains. First, newly discovered bones are washed with care then laid out on a medical table. Next, meticulous analysis and exhumation site photographs help to determine if the remains are of one or more individuals. Commingled bones are then separated and a three-part biological profile undertaken to determine each deceased person's sex, stature and approximate age. Teeth (if any) are checked for distinctive dental work and a forensic pathological examination looks for old, distinguishing broken bones or signs of childhood illness. Possessions such as rings, combs, watches, cigarette lighters and clothing are noted in an inventory.

'Once a colleague found inside a young man's wallet photographs of Elizabeth Taylor and Paul Newman,' he said. 'He must have been a romantic guy.'

'Although we try to remain distanced and not to become emotional, each case is an individual, of course,' admitted Photis. 'Once three generations of a single family were brought into the lab: a grandmother, her daughter and the daughter's nine-month-old son. In the photographs from the field we saw that the younger woman had been holding the baby in her arms, turning away from the killers, shielding her son from them. He'd been wearing a bib and a nappy. In the lab we are used to seeing big, adult bones but the baby was so small,' he said, stroking his forearm to indicate its length. 'At the time my own wife was six months pregnant with our first child...'

Photis's voice trailed off. He paused, lit a cigarette then gathered his thoughts. 'This is a small island. We are human. When we begin our examinations we are aware where the remains have been found but that information makes absolutely no difference to our work.'

Alongside the archaeologists, CMP anthropologists take part in the return of remains to families. In the onsite Family Viewing Facility, the scientists explain the process of analysis and identification to the bereaved. In most cases, the mothers of the missing choose not to attend the event. But in 2014 one family decided to bring the mother, who was in a wheelchair and had been senile for years. The woman said nothing during the detailed explanation but – when she was wheeled in to the viewing room and saw the small number of bones and the photograph of her 40-year-lost son – she suddenly started to wail with a sound of uncontrollable grief.

'Every time I see such outpouring of emotion, I realise that what I'm seeing is relief,' said Photis. 'Why? Because now the family knows. Now their loss is tangible, and at last they will have a place to weep for their lost loved one.'

Emine Çetinsel

'I have private moments with them all,' said Emine Çetinsel, 24, the youngest anthropologist and newest employee of the CMP. 'I especially take time and care when laying out the bones before the family viewing. I want to ensure that the head is positioned just right, that the reassembled skeleton is anatomically correct. This is my way of paying respect, and of saying goodbye.'

Emine grew up in the northern half of the divided capital. She was a curious and independent child, often rebellious, always arguing with her elder brother. In time her curiosity for the world became focused on a fascination with forensic science. She moved to England to study forensic science and criminal investigation at Central Lancashire University. When she returned to Cyprus for the summer holidays she started an internship at CMP and later was offered the job.

'I realised immediately how much I loved the work: studying evidence, assembling information,' she said, talking with infectious enthusiasm. 'I find it fascinating to read the bones. In them one can see evidence of an accident, for example. One can tell if a man was a smoker or if a woman had given birth, or spot childhood vitamin deficiencies, or rickets, or even detect a limp. By gathering such insights, we naturally begin to imagine what the individual was like when he or she was alive.'

Remarkably Emine helped to identify her missing grandfather.

'On 23 December 1963 my grandfather, a road works supervisor, left for work and never came home,' she said with an intensity that suggested she had been with him on the day of his disappearance... 30 years before her birth. 'My grandmother cried all night. She had heard that roadblocks had been set up in Nicosia and that he'd been stopped and taken away. Two nights later paramilitaries came to the house looking for him. My grandmother shouted at them, "I should ask you that question. You've already arrested him." The men then took away my father's brother instead.'

In 2013 the CMP began to excavate a redundant well in Kokkinotrimithia, a town of 4,000 inhabitants that lies to the west of Nicosia. When the remains of five bodies were found and brought into the lab, Emine began to suspect that one of them might be her grandfather.

'As the bones were being washed, I remembered that my grandmother had often mentioned Kokkinotrimithia. She'd always had a strange idea that he had been taken to a kind of prison camp there.'

Coincidentally that evening Emine's mother – who had been five years old when her father had gone missing – asked Emine if any bones had been found that day.

'Last night I had a dream about their discovery,' the older woman confessed to Emine.

'Don't be crazy, Mum,' replied Emine, hardly believing her ears.

Six months later, after DNA testing and the completion of the anthropological analysis, Emine's suspicions were confirmed. A colleague in the lab said to her, 'Come and meet your grandfather.'

'The discovery brought closure for my family, even though my grandmother didn't want to see her husband's bones. Some people want to touch the remains, to hold a hand, even to kiss the skull. But most people prefer either to stay in the adjoining room, or to stare at the table from the doorway.'

On the eve of Kurban Bayramı, the religious holiday during the Islamic month Dhu'l-Hijjah, Emine and her mother – in common with almost everyone in the north of Cyprus – visit the graves of deceased relatives. In a Nicosia cemetery the two women pray at the end of the row of 20 white marble tombs. Emine lays fresh flowers on the grave and lights a stick of incense, its slim, scented spiral of smoke rising into the pine trees.

'My mother remembers nothing about her father,' admitted Emine. 'Her first ever Father's Day with him was here at the graveside earlier this year.'

Their loss isn't confined to one side of the family. Sometimes the family also visits Emine's father's long-deserted village – Süleymaniye or Agios Ioannis – which lies in the far west of the island in the no-man's-land within the Buffer Zone.

'Once my father's village exported the finest figs to Australia,'

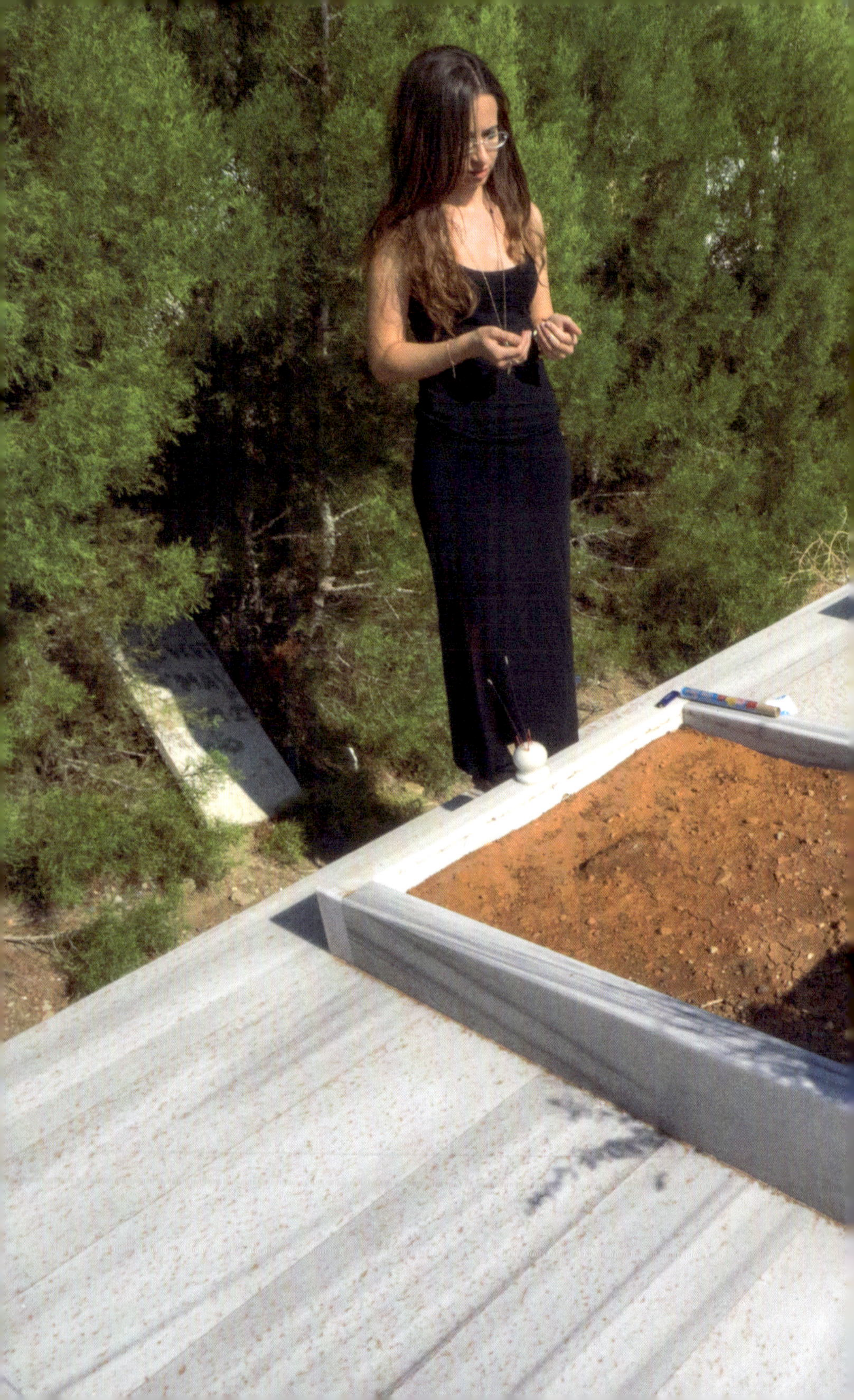

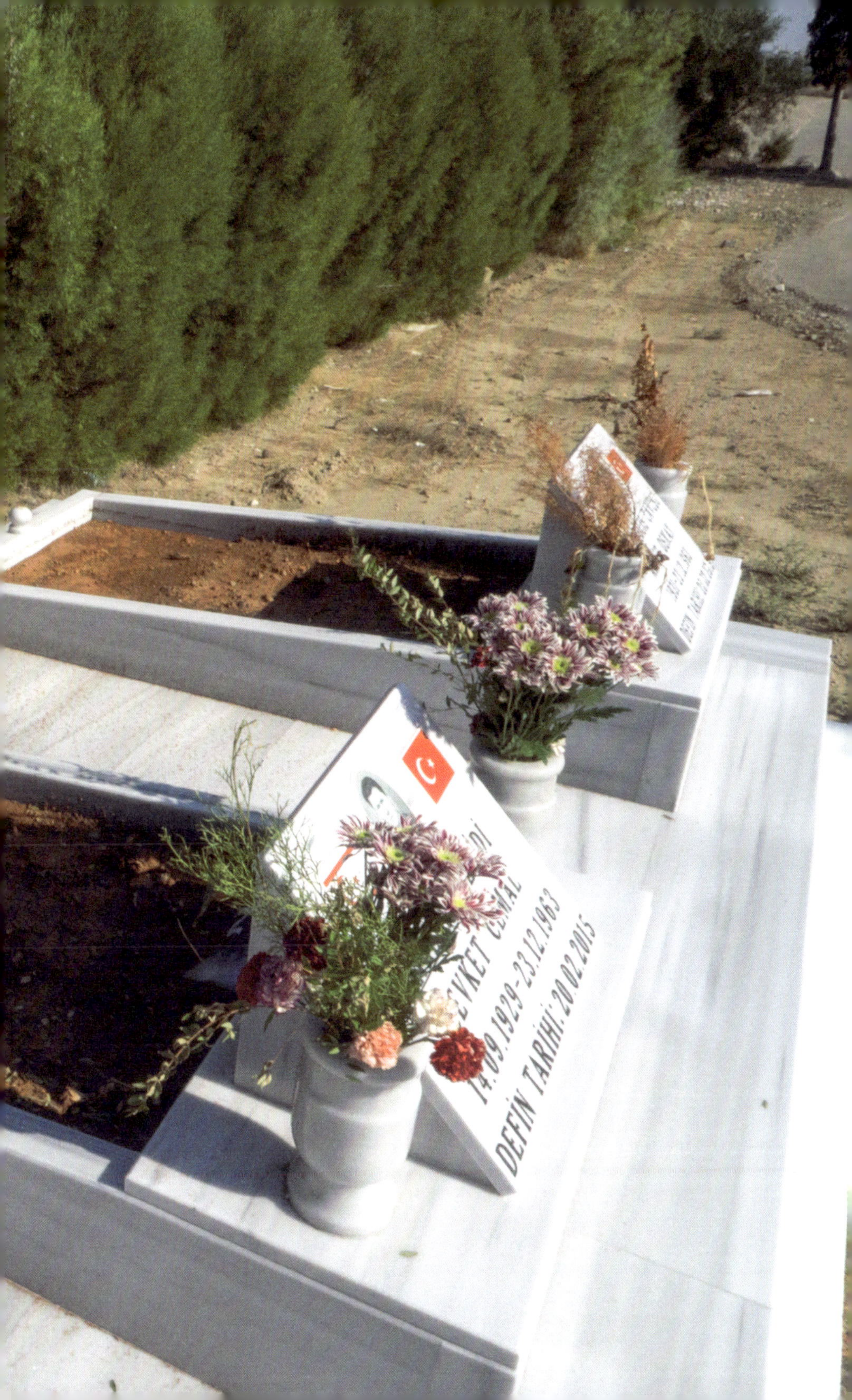
EVKET CEMAL
14.09.1929-23.12.1963
DEFİN TARİHİ: 20.02.2015

she said. 'Today we need permission from the UN to visit it, and then we are allowed only for a few hours and to pick mushrooms.' She paused, thinking of the vanished village where she might have grown up, and said, 'The air is so fresh there that you can almost feel the oxygen.'

'I wouldn't do this work if I didn't love it,' Emine said later. 'I am really happy that it was me who analysed – and then cared for – my grandfather. As to whether this work is important or not, I often think that the two communities don't consider it of much value... apart of course from the individuals who lost someone. But then after all, the CMP is about individuals.'

Previous pages:
Emine Çetinsel helped to identify the remains of her grandfather, as have other CMP employees. 'We knew that he was dead of course. But now finally there is a grave for him, and he can rest,' she said at his graveside. She added, 'As you see, it was a bit of luck that I became a forensic scientist.'

In the summer days of childhood, Maria-Chrystalla Kyrkimtzi's mother often visited her favourite beach in the northern part of the island. But for recent decades that beach has been all but inaccessible to her. Today Maria-Chrystalla has found her own beach, in the south.

Maria-Chrystalla Kyrkimtzi

'Whenever I come back to Cyprus, I go to my beach,' said Maria-Chrystalla Kyrkimtzi, 30, spreading the tobacco over the rolling paper, reaching for a filter. 'It's not a particularly popular place. There is no sand and it's no good for swimming. I don't even remember how I first discovered it. But after university, or after a holiday, I like to go there to sit and watch the waves, to think of what I've done, and what I will do with my life.' She rolled her cigarette then paused, and added, 'It is my special place.'

Maria-Chrystalla's mother is a Cypriot. Her father is Greek. She grew up in Thessaloniki, spending every summer on the island, knowing that she had two nationalities, feeling at home in both places.

'Sometimes I told people that I was from Greece, other times I'd say that I was from Cyprus. It depended on the circumstances. This is my heritage.'

At the age of 18, Maria-Chrystalla chose to study history and archaeology in Cyprus. Even though she had known the island all her life, she found living much different than on the Greek mainland.

'Night comes earlier in Cyprus,' she explained with a laugh. 'In Greece 8pm is considered late afternoon. The evening starts when one meets friends for a drink at 10pm. Here 8pm is evening.

Life is quieter on Cyprus and people are more conservative, more careful in their jokes and small talk. They don't want to be caught talking about someone you may know. This is a small community.'

After earning her BSc. at the University of Cyprus, Maria-Chrystalla moved to Edinburgh to do her Masters. She lived in a hall of residence on the Royal Mile, awoke to the sound of bagpipes and – during the Festival – watched the evening fireworks and Royal Tattoo from her window. In the UK she focused on human osteoarchaeology, the study of human bones in an archaeological (or historical) context. The warmth of the Scots compensated for the dire weather and her sense of loneliness, but nothing could bring her to terms with the early winter nightfall.

In 2009 Maria-Chrystalla returned home to take up a post at the Cyprus Institute. Although she enjoyed the work on ancient remains, it seemed to lack relevance. When the opportunity arose to join the CMP, she seized the chance.

'Although the methodology is similar, I feel that the CMP's work has more purpose and meaning. Above all, meeting the families of the missing is so moving for me.'

As a CMP anthropologist, Maria-Chrystalla analyses human remains to determine age, sex and height and so create a biological profile. She also examines the bones for evidence of perimortem trauma: gunshot wounds, blast or blunt force injuries. She details any surviving personal objects: a wallet, a Christian cross, a star and crescent necklace. She takes bone samples for DNA analysis and – once the results are known – brings together all the available data in preparation for the return of the remains.

'I was very nervous the first few times I met the bereaved,' she recalled, keeping her emotions in check. 'Inevitably the return of the remains is a heartbreaking experience.'

Often during the viewing of the remains there is anger. Always there is weeping. Once a mother stood over her son's bones and sang a lament that she'd composed over years, bringing the gathered family and scientists to tears. But always in the end there is a silence.

Maria-Chrystalla looked down at her hands and said, 'I often think that it's in those quiet moments that people are most hurting.'

She rolled the cigarette back and forth in her long fingers, then went on, 'Our work is belittled from time to time. Some critics ask why we don't just leave the dead to lie in peace? Or say that we shouldn't bother as there is no legal follow-up. To my mind we do it for the relatives. The relatives simply need to know – have a right to know – what happened to their loved ones all those years ago.'

Maria-Chrystalla is a quiet, independent young woman with fine, symmetrical features. She wears a simple silver necklace and intricate coiled silver ring. She lives alone in Nicosia's old town, with a parakeet.

'The bird has no name,' she admitted. 'In fact it's not even mine. A few years ago my little cousin asked me to look after it, and I agreed because it needed a home. But to be honest I'm a bit afraid of birds. Once I thought of setting it free but I couldn't do it of course. It is my responsibility to look after the bird.'

Today Maria-Chrystalla rarely leaves the island, and rarely visits her special beach.

'I never have time now. Life has become too busy but – even if years pass until my next visit – it feels like a place that I have always known, and that will always be mine.'

Genetic Phase

Genetic analysis and bone profiling is key for the identification and association of skeletal elements. Bone DNA is compared with the genetic profiles of the relatives of the missing. A bone and blood match of at least 99.95% accuracy is required for a result to be considered a positive identification.

Over the last decade the collection of blood samples from relatives of the Turkish Cypriot missing persons has been carried out by the Turkish Cypriot DNA Laboratory at the Dr. Burhan Nalbantoğlu Hospital. The Cyprus Institute of Neurology and Genetics (CING) carried out similar DNA extraction and profiling of the relatives of Greek Cypriot missing persons over the same period of time.

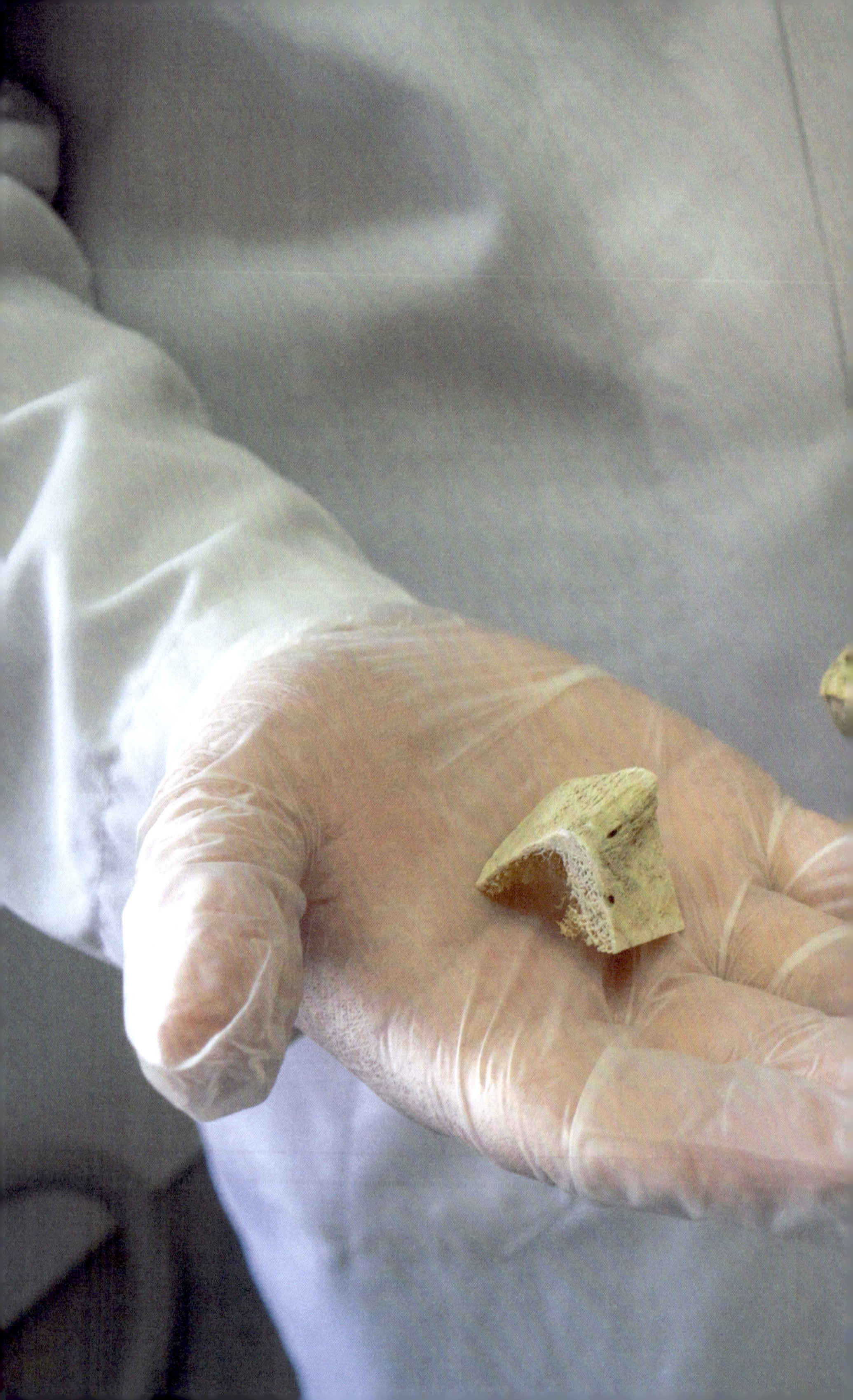

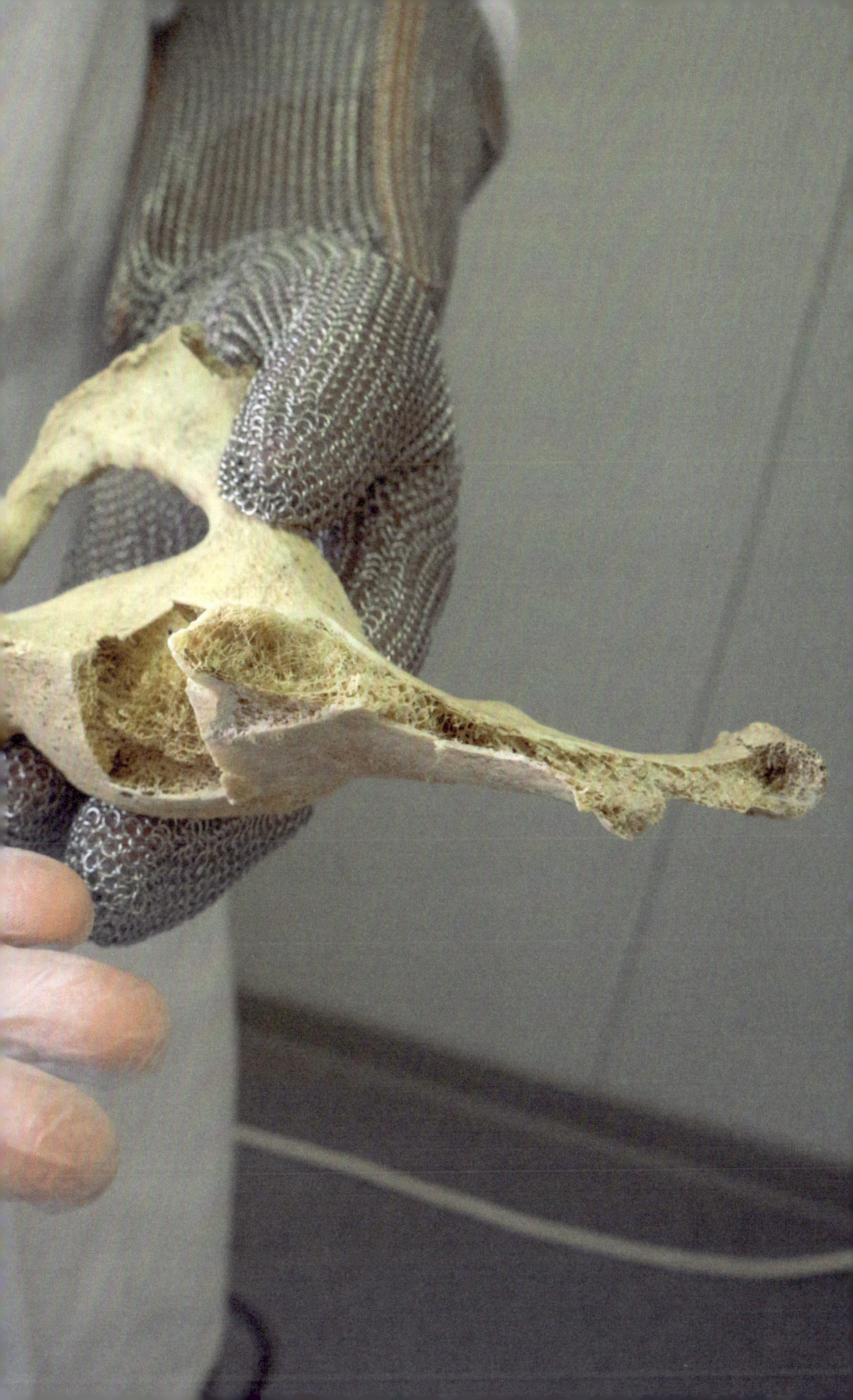

To identify human remains with certainty, a genetic match must be made between the bones of the deceased and the blood or saliva of their close relatives. To this end a small bone sample – ideally taken from the femur – is cut and sent abroad to a specialist laboratory to extract the deceased person's DNA.

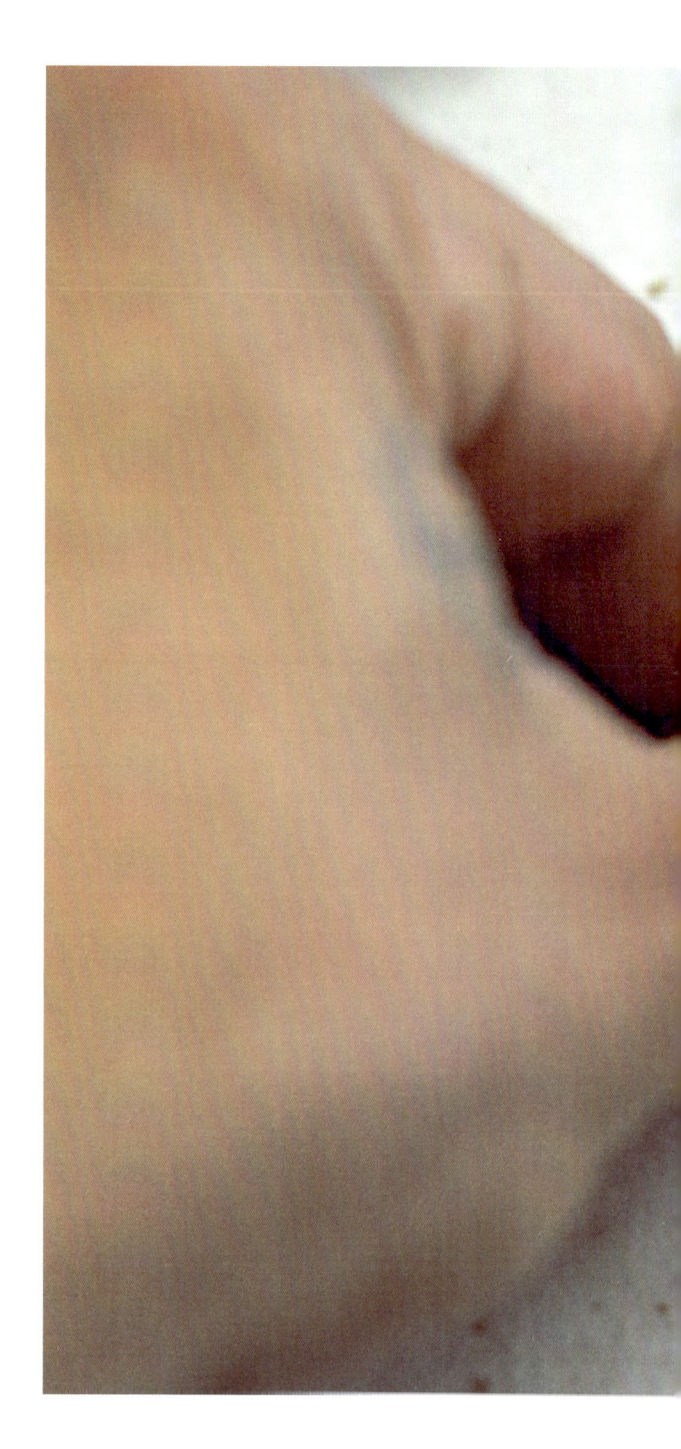

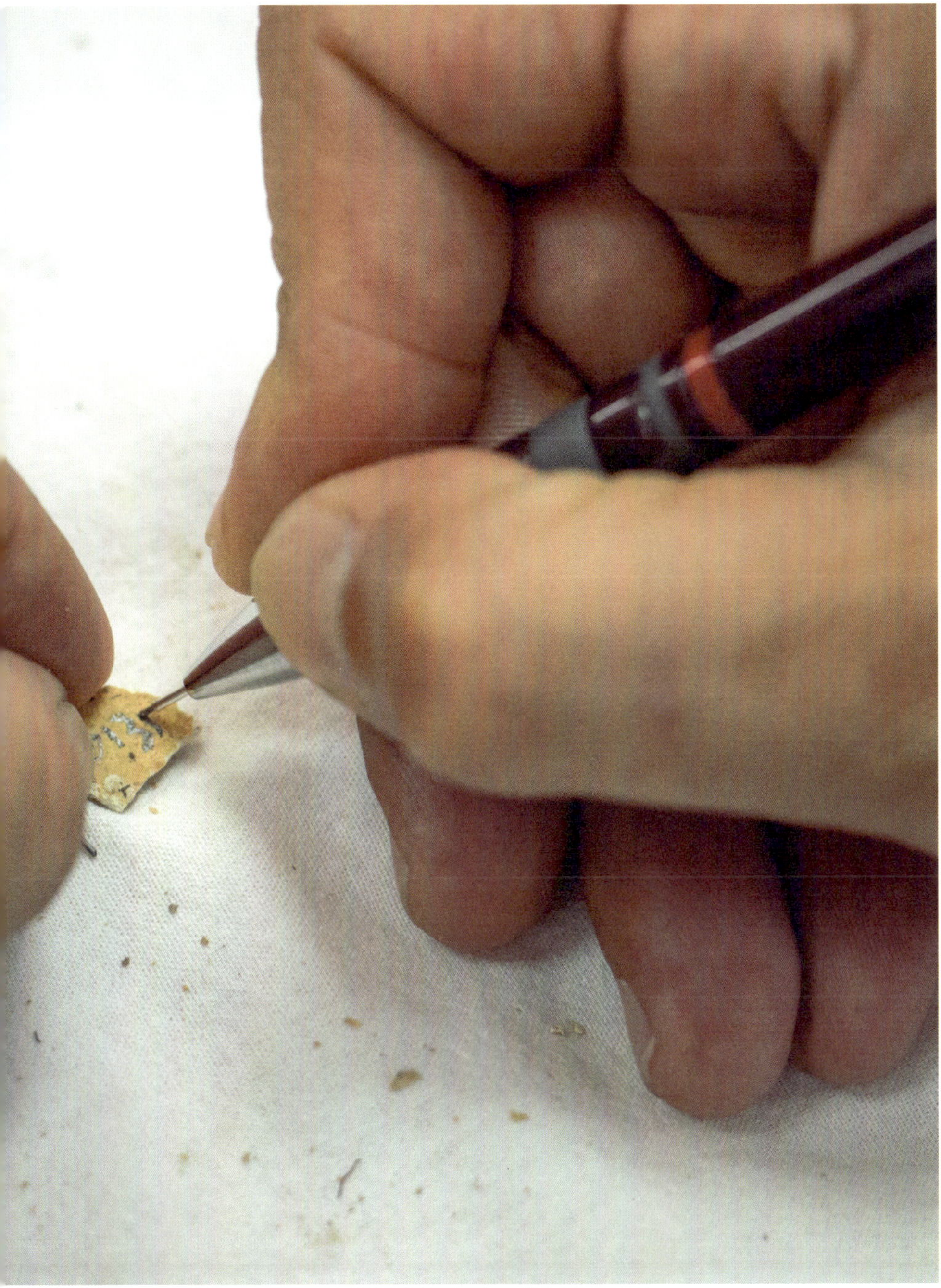

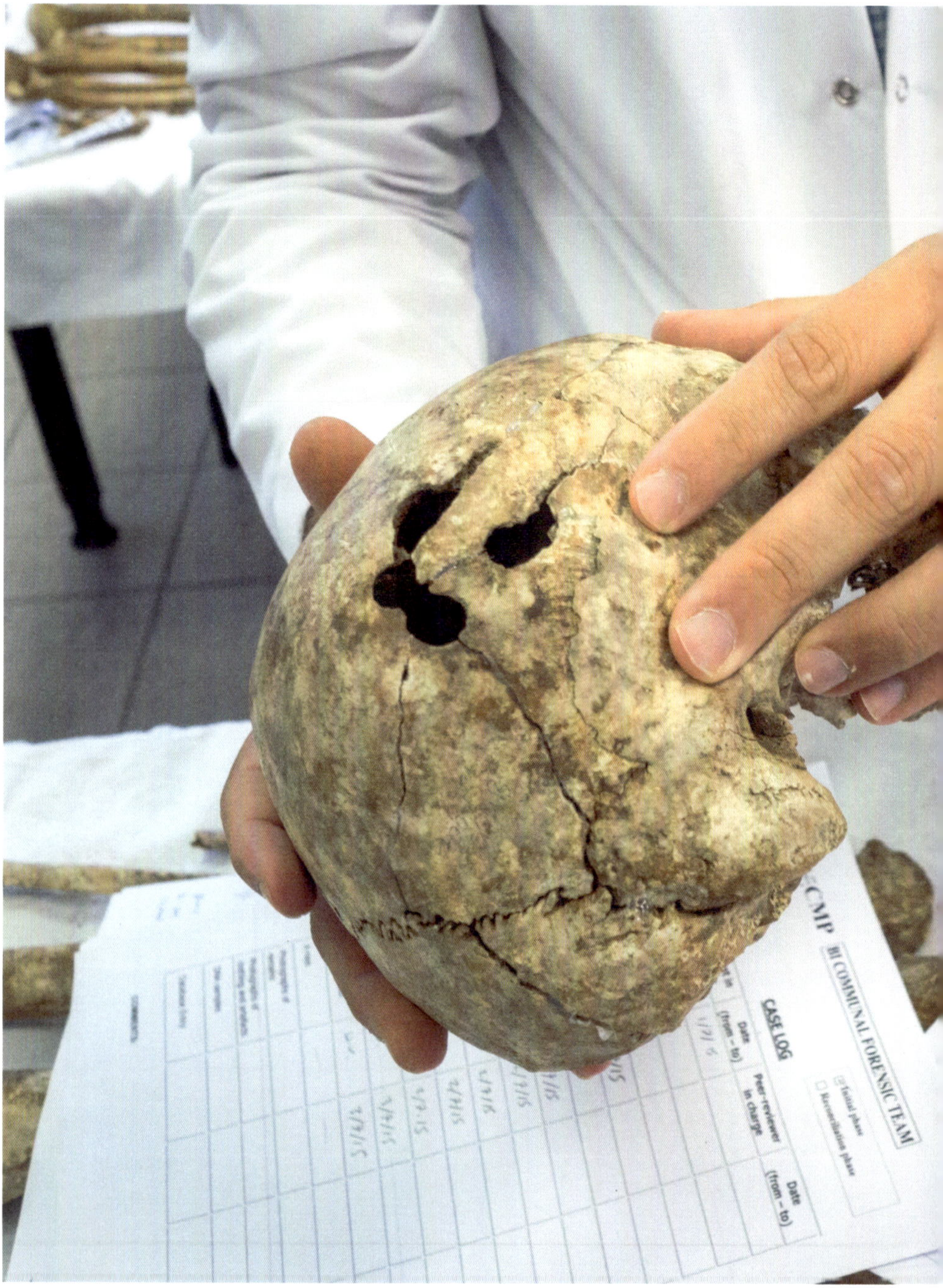
CMP BI-COMMUNAL FORENSIC TEAM
CASE LOG
Date (from – to)
Peer-reviewer in charge
Date (from – to)

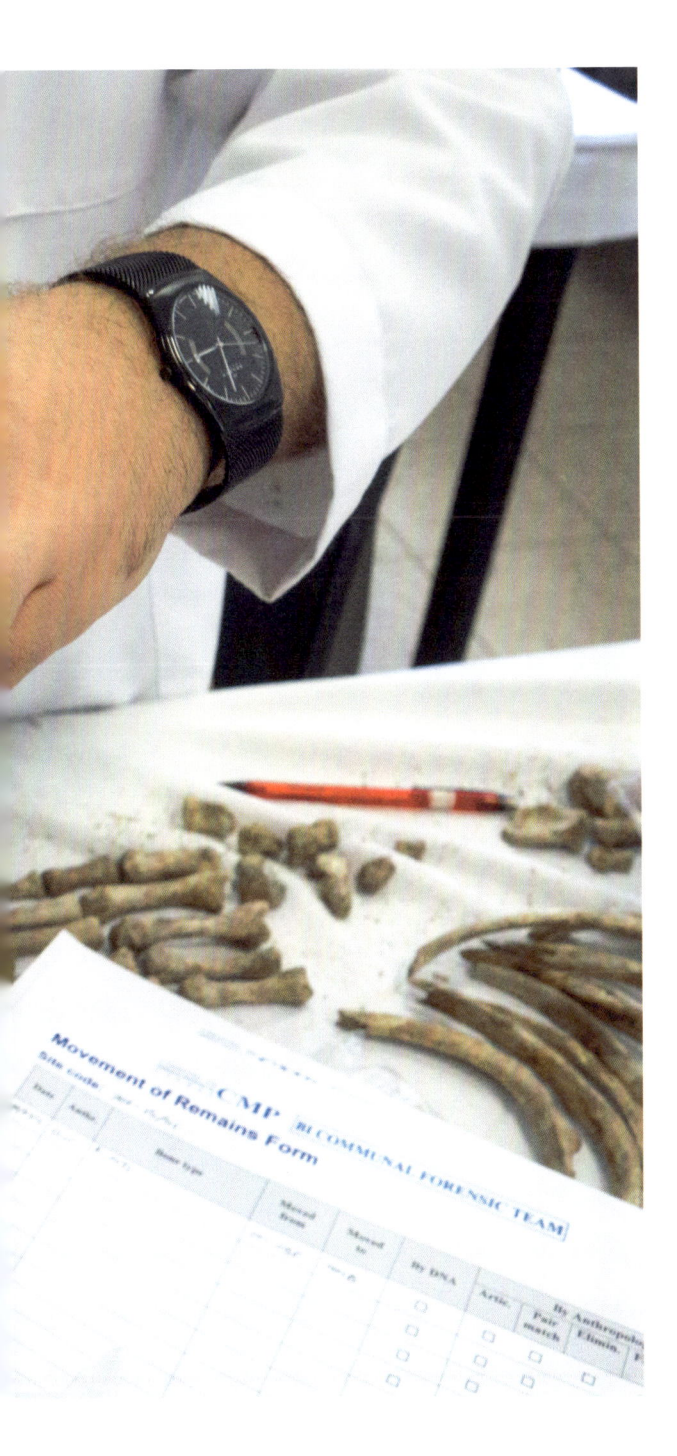

A CMP comprehensive report, compiled in preparation for final identification, does not record traumas related to the cause of death, even if it is obvious. The anthropologist reports only 'what can be seen on the bones'. Often the bereaved simply want to know if their son, father or sister had suffered, and if the end had been swift.

Following pages:
In some cases, small bones may no longer contain DNA as it can be destroyed by burning or years of exposure to harsh sunlight. Nevertheless such unidentified remains are stored at the CMP Anthropological Laboratory in anticipation of future advances in DNA science.

604-11/17-014GBP

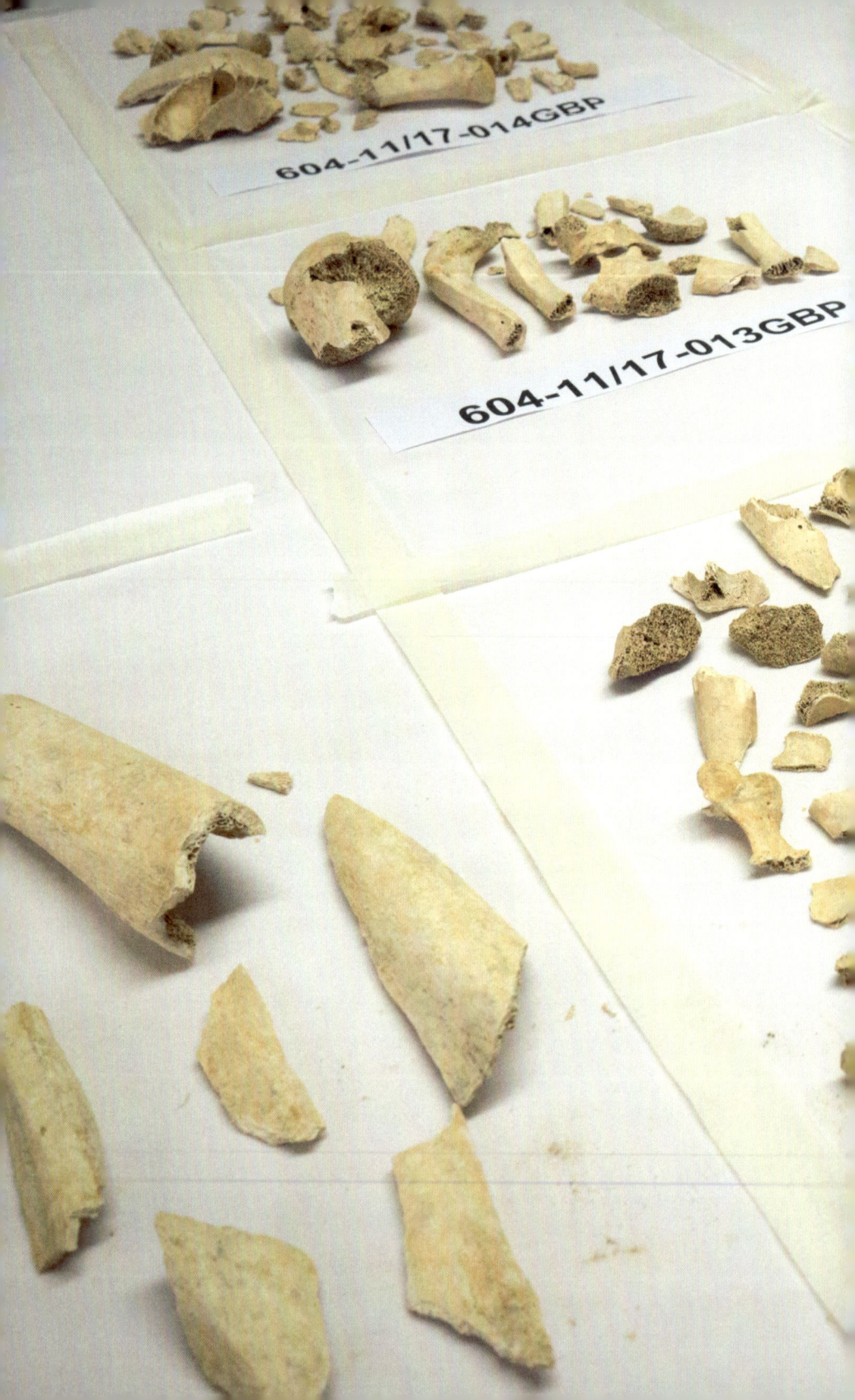

604-11/17-013GBP

604-11/17-017GBP

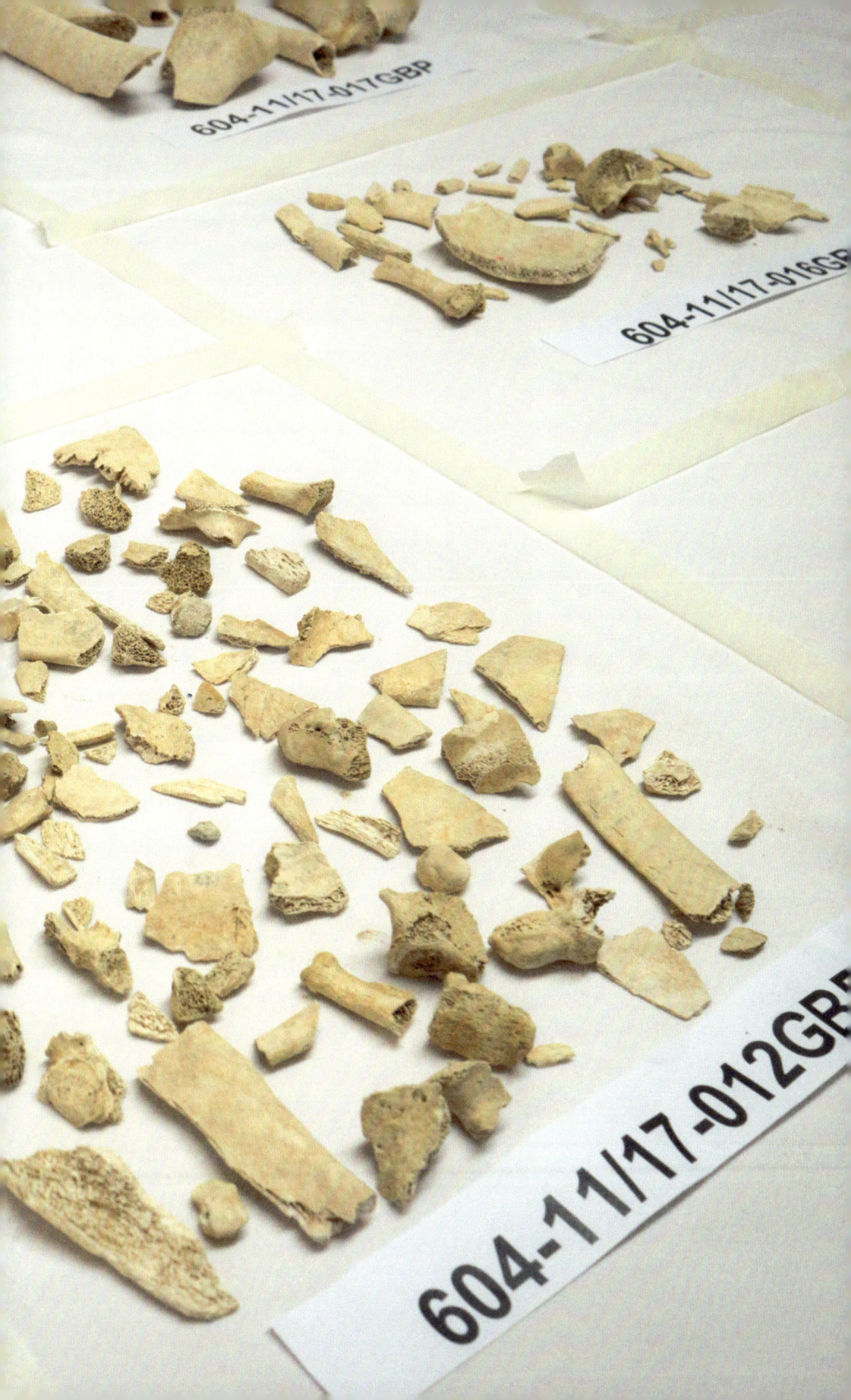

604-11/17-016GBP

604-11/17-012GBP

Every step of the process is documented in detail, in the laboratory as in the field. Here Duygu Göze, a CMP forensic photographer, records the sampling of a thigh bone, using the individual's anonymous identification number established at the gravesite.

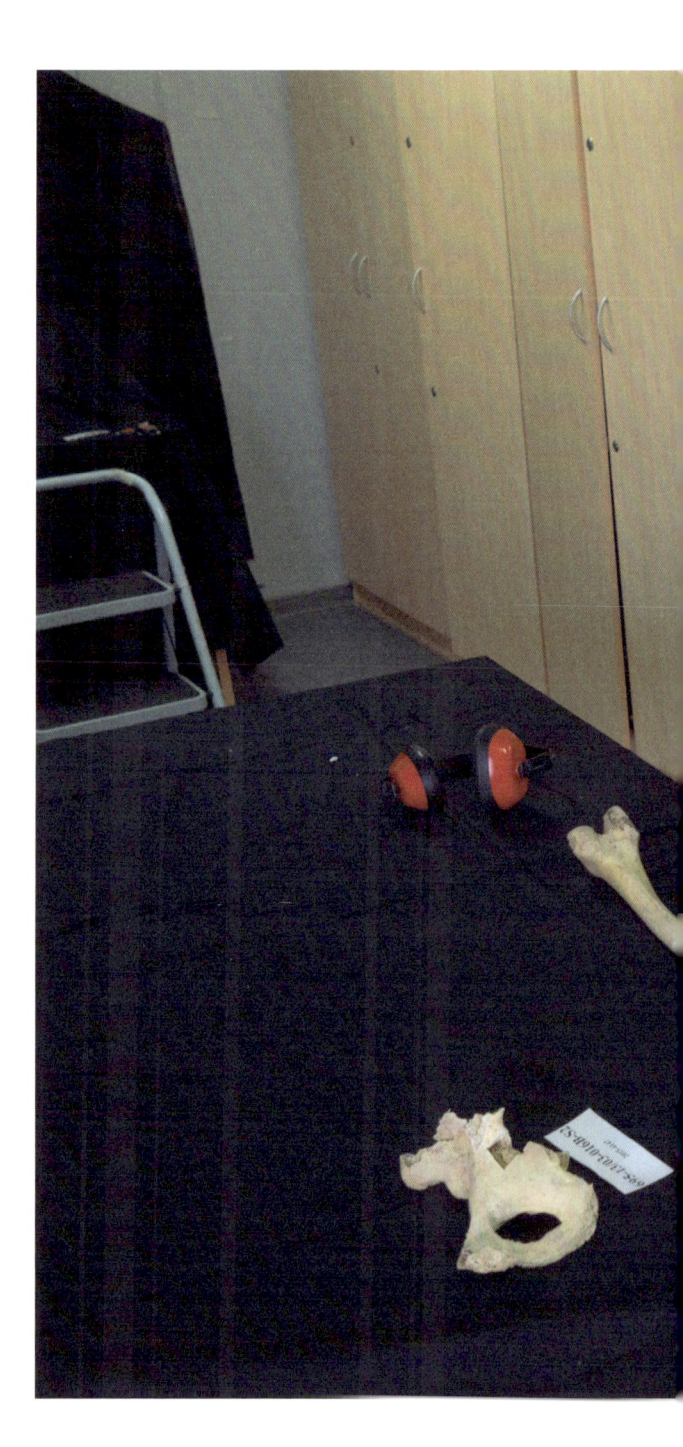

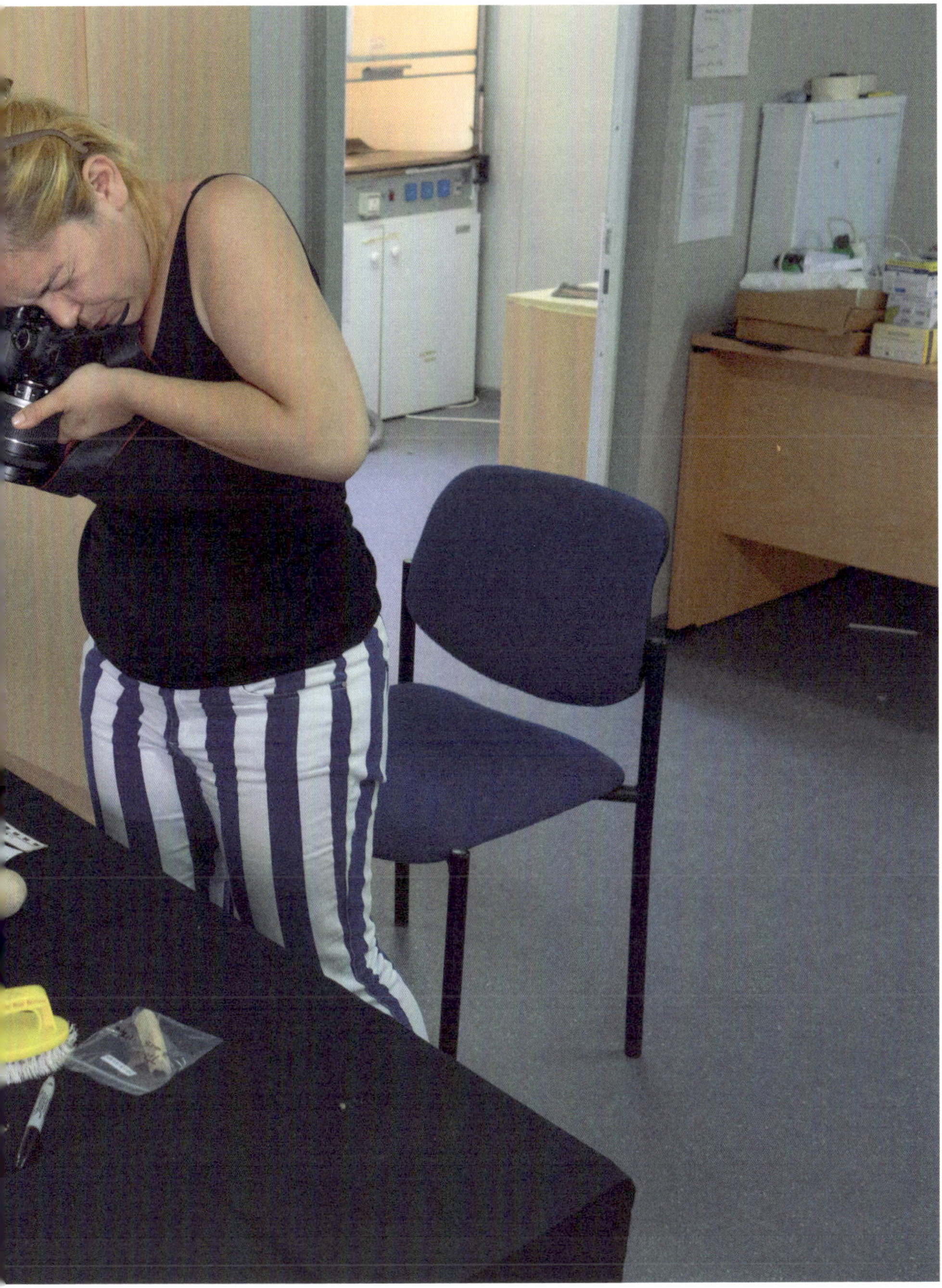

İstenç Engin is leader of the second team at the CMP Anthropological Laboratory. 'Our work is important for the bereaved families of course, some of whom have been waiting 40 or 50 years for closure. But it's also important because it helps people on both sides to understand that both parties hurt each other, and that they have the same pain, and that they are both guilty.'

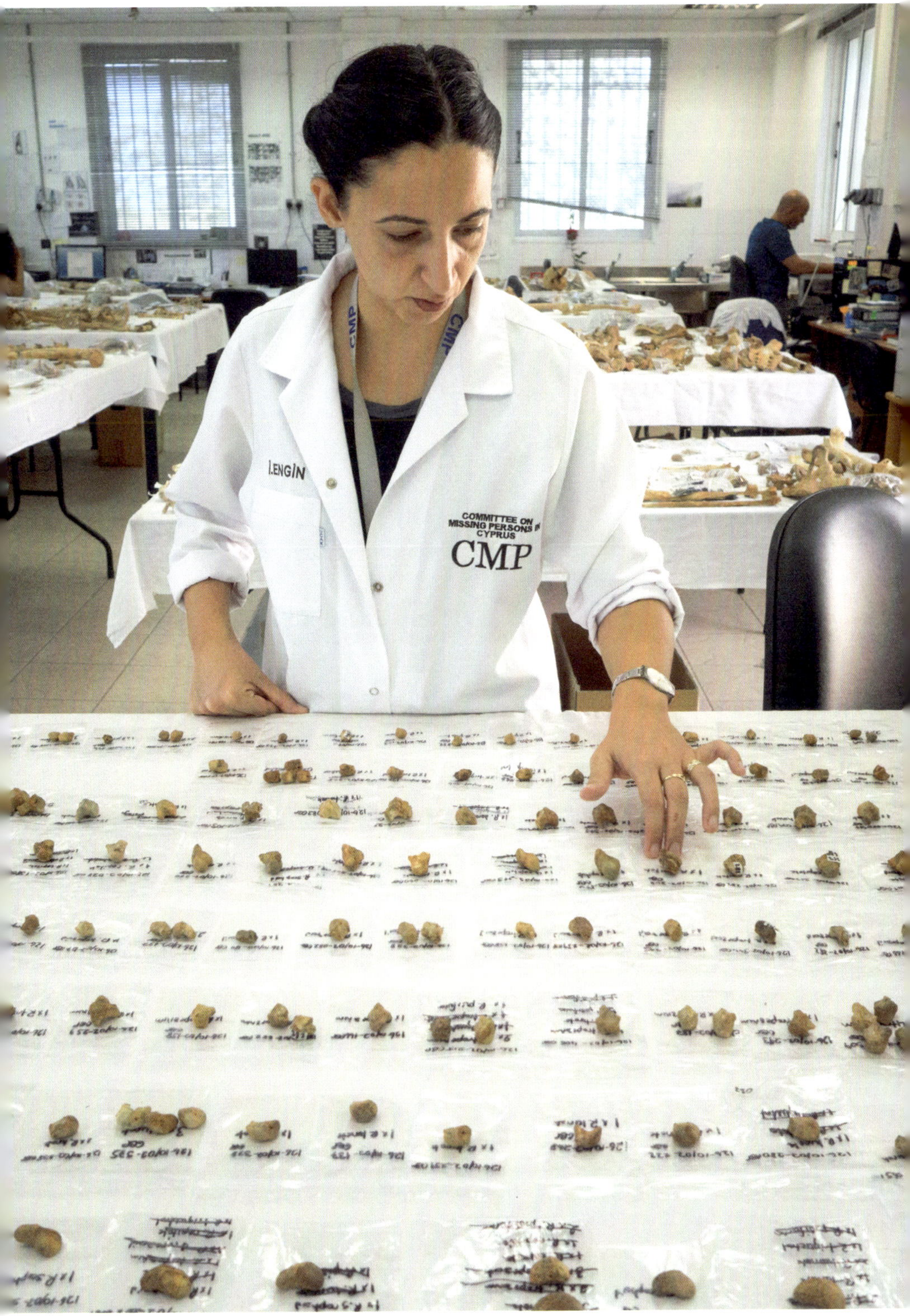
COMMITTEE ON
MISSING PERSONS IN
CYPRUS
CMP

US-trained geneticist Gülbanu Zorba – alongside her Greek Cypriot counterpart Katerina Papaioannou – verifies the matching of DNA extracted from bones with DNA obtained from family blood or saliva samples.

Gülbanu Zorba

In Cyprus almost everyone is related, went to school together or fought together. Gülbanu Zorba, 32, is a lively and elegant geneticist. Her father and her husband's uncle were at the same university. She and her husband's brother went to the same primary school. Once on a weekend mountain walk on the far side of the island, a stranger stopped Gülbanu and told her, 'You are Ilkay's daughter. You look just like your mother did when she was your age. She and I were friends at high school.'

'Cyprus is a small country and this can be a challenge for DNA identification,' said Gülbanu, tucking her long, fine black hair behind an ear. 'Our original villages were small, consisting of small numbers of families. The same Y chromosome is passed down the male line for generations. If four sons of one woman have gone missing, it is not possible to differentiate them by DNA with only a reference sample from their mother.'

At the CMP Gülbanu's job, like that of Katerina Papaioannou, her Greek Cypriot counterpart in the bi-communal Forensic Genetics Team, is to identify individuals through genetics. After school in Nicosia she won a scholarship to study at the University of Missouri-Kansas City – where she came top of her year – then moved on to Houston's Baylor College of Medicine to join its renowned human genetic programme.

'But after six years in the States I realised that I missed home too much. One of my cousins had married, and I hadn't been there. Another cousin had had his first child, and I hadn't been there. My father then developed a heart condition. So I took a year's leave of absence from Baylor.'

Once home, Gülbanu decided to join the CMP, visiting the families of the missing, extracting DNA from blood samples, recording family trees and hearing stories.

'In the beginning, I was in tears every single day. During the years when the border was sealed, many of the families had believed that their loved ones were still alive in the south. When the gates opened in 2003, many expected them to come home. Night after night women prepared their husband's or son's favourite meal and waited… waited.'

Over the last decade Gülbanu and her colleagues have worked on the Family Reference Samples coded database. Through it living relatives can be linked to the dead by matching the DNA of blood and bone samples. Positive matches are double-checked with electropherograms – plots of results from analyses using an automated DNA sequencer – and linked to the reports and findings of investigators, archaeologists and anthropologists for the reconciliation meeting.

'Deep down the families of the missing know that their loved ones are dead but haven't been able to accept it,' said Gülbanu. 'They hang on to the belief that they are alive quite simply because they never saw them dead. At the Family Viewing Facility they see the bones, and cry as if their loved one had died only yesterday.'

Cypriots live with ghosts. Two relatives of Gülbanu's husband Mentes have been missing for over 50 years. In 1963 his uncle had fallen ill with appendicitis and been admitted to hospital. His grandfather had driven to Nicosia to see his son.

'No one knows what then happened to them,' said Mentes, standing beside his wife in their new Nicosia home. 'We heard that my uncle was taken from his bed and shot in the hospital before being buried. However that is only a rumour. We do not know the reality. My grandfather also went missing, along with his car.' Mentes paused then added, 'We hope for peace in Cyprus, for reconciliation.'

Around their feet tottered their three-and-a-half-year-old daughter Azra, trying out her mother's high heels. Azra means 'untouched pearl' in old Turkish.

'We are Cypriots and we want our daughter to be a Cypriot,' said Gülbanu. 'What does that mean? It means that we are islanders, that we have our own culture.'

As Azra tipped off the high heels and onto the marble floor, Gülbanu scooped her up and embraced her. Mentes – an environmental engineer – then recounted his last visit to the UK.

'In London I met two Cypriot shopkeepers. Their shops were

next door to each other on Green Lanes in Haringey. They were from the same village and were friends, even though one was a Greek Cypriot and the other a Turkish Cypriot. "Why can't Cypriots be like this at home?" I asked them.'

Identification and Return of Remains

In the Reconciliation of Information Phase, ante-mortem data and reports from the investigative teams are compared with the post-mortem data and DNA results obtained from the anthropological and genetic analyses. If information is consistent and no discrepancies come to light, the CMP Identification Coordinator formally identifies the remains of a missing person. The respective Cypriot Member of the Committee then informs the family and offers them the chance to meet the scientists and to view the remains. Finally the remains of the identified individual are returned to the relatives, who receive a contribution towards funeral costs. Through this last phase of the process, a team of psychologists from each community helps families to come to terms with their loss.

Following pages:
Nazire Sadık Çelebi was 101 years old in 1964 when fighting erupted in the vicinity of the remote village of Küçük Selçuklu/Ayios Georgios. Her family took the children to safety, promising to return early the next day to save Nazire. But they could not come back. The CMP recovered her remains in 2012 from the ruins of her burned house. In 2016 she was buried by her 70-year-old great grandson, Nazım Cemil Kızılbora, on the right, and other surviving family members.

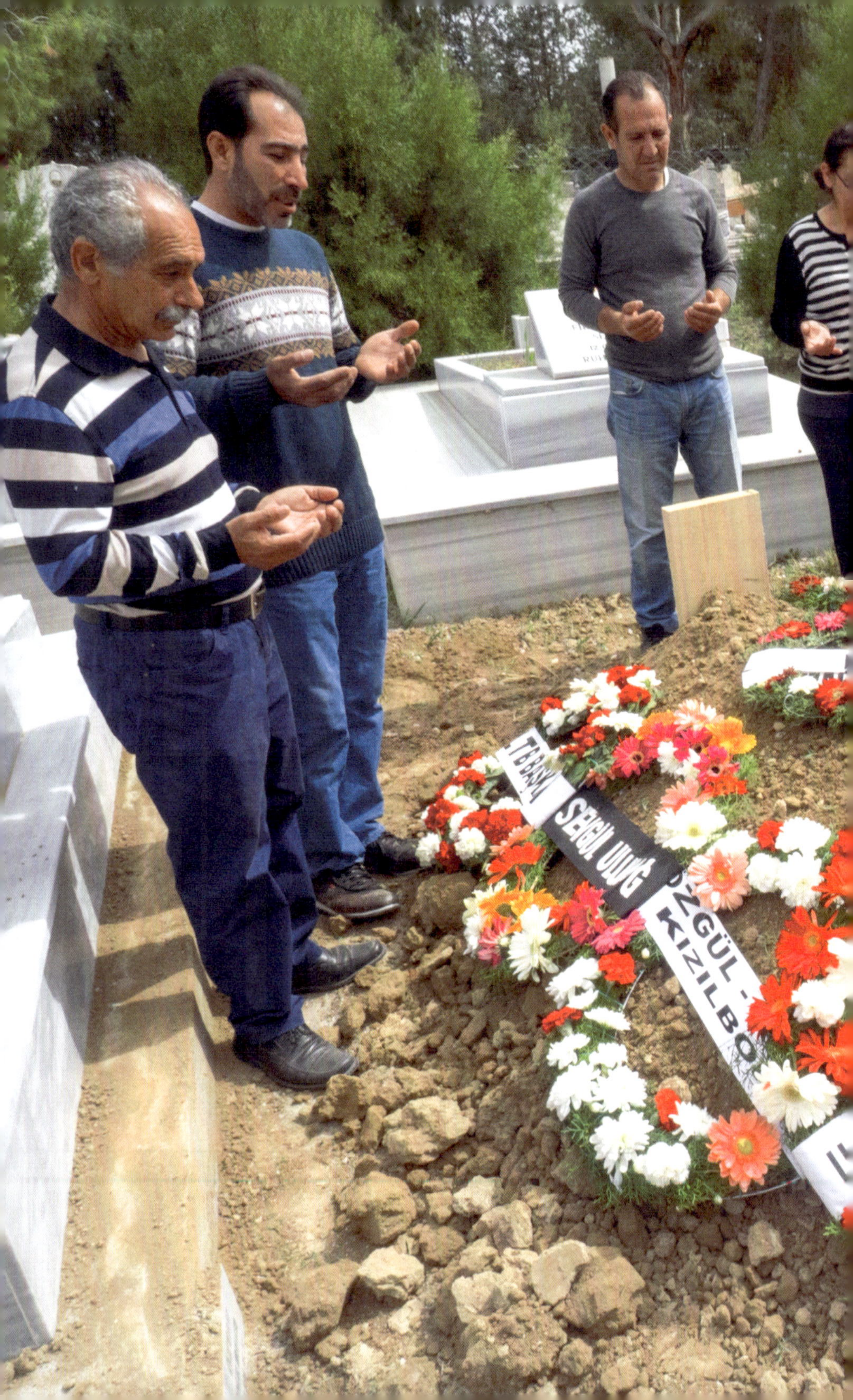

NAZİRE
SADIK
ÇELEBİ
AĞUSTOS, 1964
ŞEHİT AİLELERİ
MAL.GAZ.DE.
BİRLİK PARTİSİ

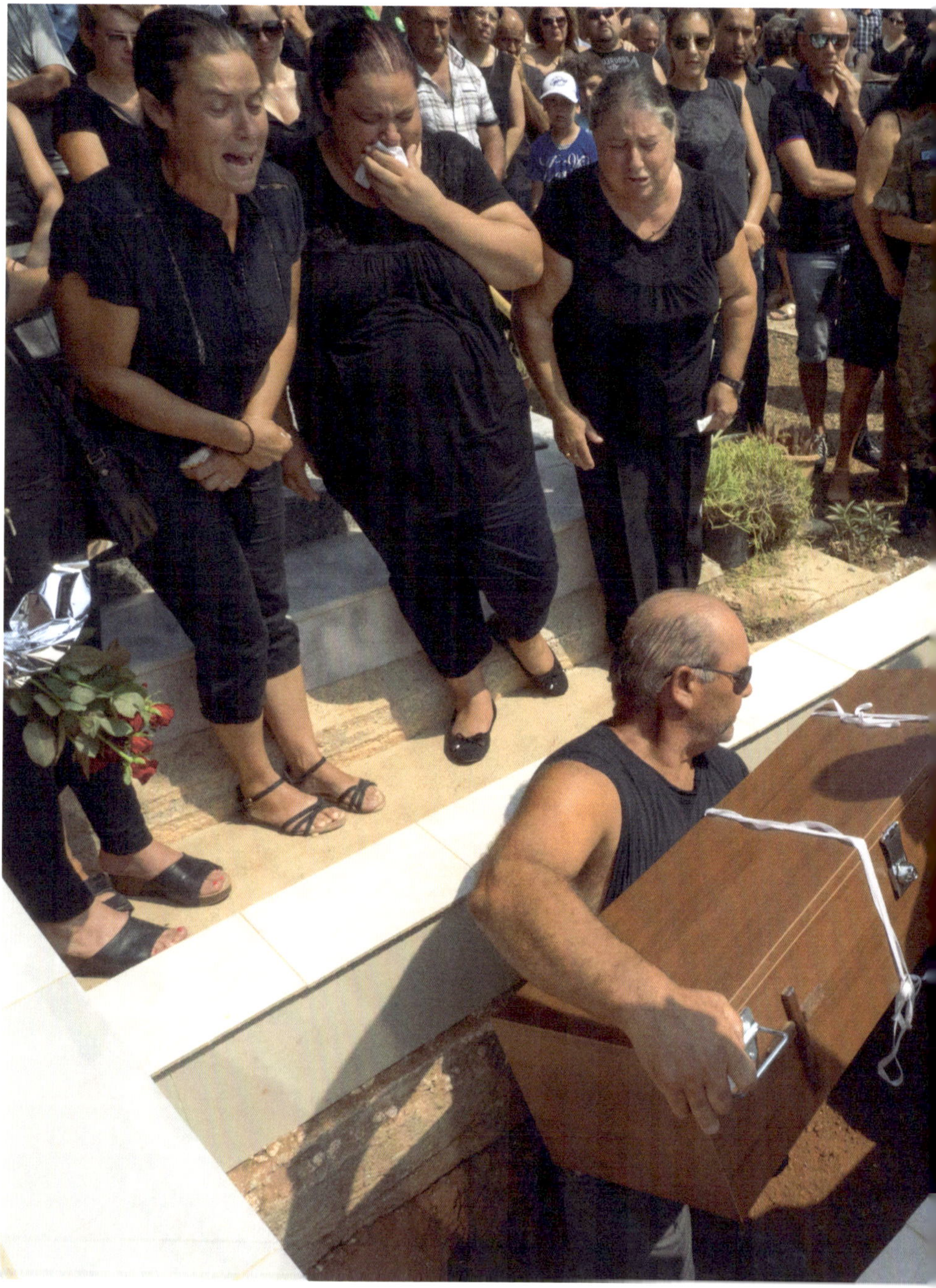

A young Cypriot, killed decades earlier, is mourned and accompanied to his grave by his four sisters and two brothers. His remains were identified by a 99.95% certain DNA match, as well as personal belongings including yellow socks, black boots and distinctive buttons.

ΑΚΟΣ ΤΖΙΑΠΡΑΣ
ΟΥΜΕΝΟΣ ΤΟΥ 1974
ΕΤΩΝ 20
ΧΑΜΠΟΥ ΤΖΙΑΠΡΑ
08-08-2012
ΕΤΩΝ 80

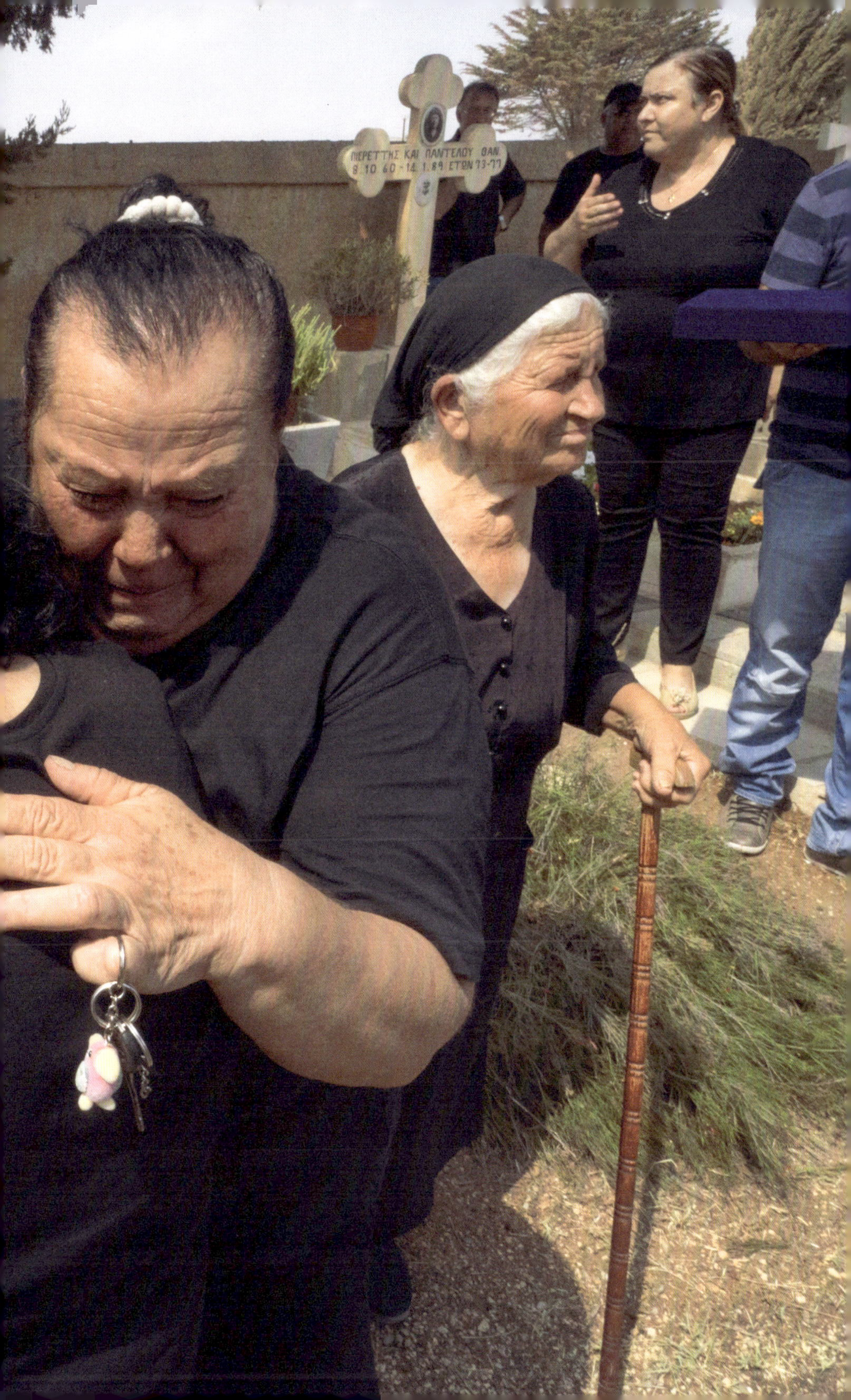
ΠΙΕΡΕΤΤΗΣ ΚΑΙ ΠΑΝΤΕΛΟΥ ΘΑΝ

Liza Zamba, one of four CMP psychologists, comforts the bereaved throughout the process of identification and final burial. After so many years of waiting for news, funerals reopen old wounds that – if accompanied with professional care – can be closed for good.

Liza Zamba

'My day might begin with a notification visit,' said Liza Zamba, a 33-year-old CMP psychologist. 'In some villages when I arrive to notify the family I find as many as 20 or 30 relatives waiting with the family to hear the news. I'll tell them that their father, mother, brother or sister has been identified. I'll see the agony in their eyes. I'll listen to them. I'll let them cry. I'll empathise with the family.'

Liza paused to draw breath.

'Or my day might begin at the Family Viewing Facility where a family will be informed of the anthropological, archaeological and DNA analysis. In this way a family will have the opportunity to understand the identification process. Those are the hardest days. One of our archaeologists, an anthropologist, the geneticist and I will share everything we know with the family. But it is never enough. The family always wants to know more. The bones only reveal so much and we can't tell them the cause of death, only that there is evidence of gunshot or blunt force injury.'

Liza's voice trailed off. Her features seemed to reflect deep inner contradictions: eyes stern but compassionate, face open yet wary of more pain. She wore no jewellery except for a simple prayer rope bracelet.

'When the identification and notification process is completed then the family arranges the funeral. My colleagues and I go to as many as two or three funerals every weekend. Also people ring me at all times of the day and night. I'll always be answering and returning calls. My aim is to provide psychological support over the telephone and to give comfort. It is important for them to know that I am next to them during this process.

Pain and trauma trickle down the generations. When Liza was 15 years old, two government officials came to her home to tell the family that the remains of her uncle – an armoured corps officer missing since 1974 – had been found.

'The men were so matter-of-fact that my grandmother fainted,' she said. 'I knew that it would be better for a woman to speak to women and started to think that I wanted this role. I wanted to help people who suffered.'

As a result Liza chose to study psychology in the UK at Derby University, working at the Royal Hospital Nottingham while completing her PhD. She returned home to Cyprus as the CMP was founded, becoming one of its first two psychologists.

'In my office there was only a desk, a chair and a huge stack of files. I sat down and started reading.'

With colleagues from both communities Liza helped to design the CMP's psycho-social support programme. Over the years she has met, comforted and cared for hundreds of bereaved families.

'Of course I hear sad stories, and I empathise with the family, but I try to remind myself that our efforts bring comfort to the families, that it enables them to find some sort of peace.'

Across the island in cavernous Agios Yorgos, the largest church in Xylofagou, some 400 mourners gather for the funeral of Kyriakos 'Tsiapras' Charalampous, a local reservist soldier 40 years dead. Beneath gilded portraits of the saints, his bones lie in a cradle-size coffin, flanked by soldiers. His family weeps beside him. Politicians stand to the right of the priests, stepping forward to add their voices to the amplified liturgy. A television cameraman changes angle for a close-up.

An honour guard then escorts the coffin as it is carried down the aisle, into the blazing September sunshine and onto a National Guard light troop transporter. The mourners surge behind it, through the narrow village lanes to the cemetery. As Kyriakos' remains are lowered back into the earth, his sisters keen themselves into hysterics, wailing in a free verse myroloi dirge

> 'Every evening our mother waited for you,
> Waited for you to walk up the road and come home...'

The old woman who was his mother never knew of her son's fate, for she died two years before the discovery of his bones.

A volley is fired over the mourners' heads and the last post is sounded. Liza moves through the crowd to stand with the family, whispering to them, embracing them. Uniformed officers also pay their respects as the soil is eased onto the coffin, burying Kyriakos for the second time in his life.

In 1974 Kyriakos Charalampous was captured along with seven other soldiers, never to be seen alive again. His remains were found in a mass grave on the other side of the island.

'Why do I do this work?' asked Liza later that day. Because I want to help people to resume their lives after the identification of their family member. Families of missing persons go through stages of anger, sadness, agony, but they have not grieved in all these years. We are next to them to help them to express their emotions and face their feelings through the grieving process. Our role is to help them to express all these suppressed feelings as I believe that unresolved grieving can lead to complications such as depression, anxiety and health problems.'

But the work weighs heavily on her. To cope with the profound secondary stress, Liza bakes biscuits, cooks and practises yoga. At the end of every day she also tries to find the time to walk in Athalassas Park where her family once gathered for Sunday picnics, and send a message or photograph to her father who works overseas in Dubai.

'I will not stop working on this project until it ends. And even then, I will continue to support the families whose loved ones are not yet found.'

Psychologist Zühre Akmanlar informs Suna Özikiz of the identifica-tion of her father's remains. Özikiz was four years old when her father Abdullah Haşim disappeared in 1963. 'I never had his love, never had a chance to hold him,' wept Özikiz, wrapping her arms around the empty air. 'Knowing the truth at last comforts me, and I am thankful for it.'

Zühre Akmanlar

In early 1974 Yusuf Besim and his family fled from their Paphos home in search of safety. As a talented chef, Yusuf found work across the island at Famagusta's Sakarya Hotel and quickly established himself as the best cook in the seaside town. But on 20 July while in the hotel kitchen he heard shooting in the neighbourhood. He immediately left work fearful for his family's safety. He never reached them.

Forty years on, CMP psychologist Zühre Akmanlar, 30, sipped her coffee in a Nicosia café and said, 'All my life my father – Yusuf's oldest son – shouted at me. He'd yell at the smallest thing. He'd yell when I asked him why he always overreacted. "You are my daughter and a daughter never questions her father," he shouted at me. He shut me out.'

In 1974, in fear for their lives, Yusuf's surviving family had been forced to move even further north. They had made their home near to Kyrenia in an abandoned barn which – in time – Zühre's father converted into a two-storey house. Zühre grew up there, gazing at the framed photographs of the missing, older man.

'My father could hardly say his name,' Zühre recalled, turning a curl of her copper hair in her fingers. 'But my aunt told me that my grandfather had been a big, magnanimous man, and a cook, and that Greek Cypriots had killed him.'

Zühre wanted to help her father, to draw him out of his unspoken grief.

'As a child I'd watched his behaviour. I'd recognised that he had a problem. But I didn't know how to deal with it.'

Zühre's father wanted her to become a teacher. But Zühre had set her mind on psychology and chose to study at Nicosia's Near East University. With her new learning and gentle prodding, her father began to look at himself as if in the mirror. He confessed that, after Yusuf's disappearance, he had been forced to become responsible for his mother and siblings. He was wracked by guilt for wanting to rebel against the obligation. Yet as the eldest son he'd had to accept it. Zühre even convinced him to give blood in the hope that DNA might help one day to identify Yusuf's still-missing bones.

'My friends tell me that I have a magical something in my face,' Zühre said with a humble and disarming shrug. 'All I know is that I want to help people. I want to understand them.'

Within weeks of her graduation, Zühre was asked to join the CMP. For almost ten years she and her fellow psychologists have broken news, held hands, given comfort as tears flowed again and again in the face of long pent-up grief. In old village houses and marble-floored villas, at kitchen tables and on leather sofas, they've heard countless old stories, soothed rages and answered innumerable questions about burial arrangements and mourning.

'For many families life stopped in 1963 or 1974. Even after so many years most families can't stop believing that their loved one is still alive,' said Zühre. 'Often they don't want to believe us when we tell them of a positive identification. Sometimes they refuse to believe the photographs, the DNA report, even the bones. Only if we show them the deceased's possessions – and they recognise them – do they immediately believe us.' She paused and took another slow sip of coffee. 'It is so hard to let go and move forward. But the bereaved can start a new chapter in their lives with their acceptance of the truth.'

Zühre's supervisor believes that she did not come to this job by chance, that she was predestined to do it. In common with Liza Zamba in the south of the island, Zühre tries to attend every funeral, tries to gauge each family's acceptance of the end. Also just like Liza, Zühre carries the weight of injustice on her shoulders and in her heart. She too suffers from secondary trauma, and tries to ease it by indulging her passion for dancing (salsa and cha-cha-cha) and for cooking. Like her grandfather Yusuf before her, Zühre has become an accomplished chef.

'As a child I used to pretend to cook elaborate meals, stealing my mother's pots and pans and making imaginative dishes from sand and leaves. Today I use more traditional ingredients,' she said with a disarming smile. 'My chocolate brownies are particularly popular. When I bake a batch and post a picture on Instagram, all my friends say they'll be right over. Next I'm keen to learn how to cook Chinese food.'

At night in bed she reads recipe books and dreams of experimenting with different ingredients, and maybe one day –

when the remains of all the missing have been found and returned to their families – opening a restaurant.

'I feel that I am Cypriot,' Zühre volunteered. 'Not Turkish. Not Turkish Cypriot. Simply Cypriot.' She paused, pushed back her long copper hair and added, 'You do know that in both communities the dishes that we eat are exactly the same?'

This is the 195th time that Zühre Akmanlar has handed a final report to a bereaved family member.
'It never gets easier,' she admitted. 'Trauma trickles down the generations. I believe that only after all the missing are found will Cyprus be able to finally deal with its trauma. I love my job and the work of the CMP and I hope one day they will help to find my own father.'

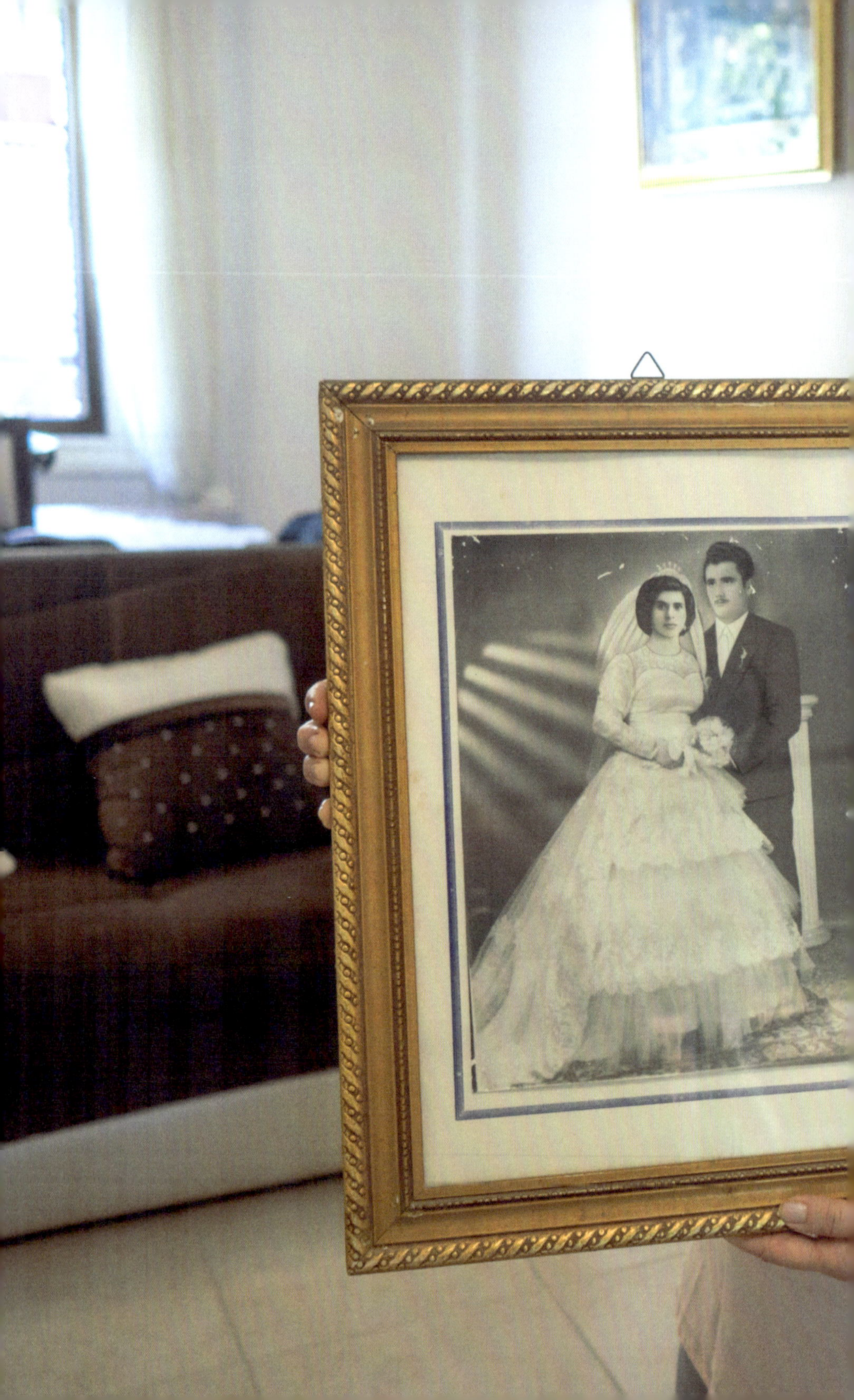

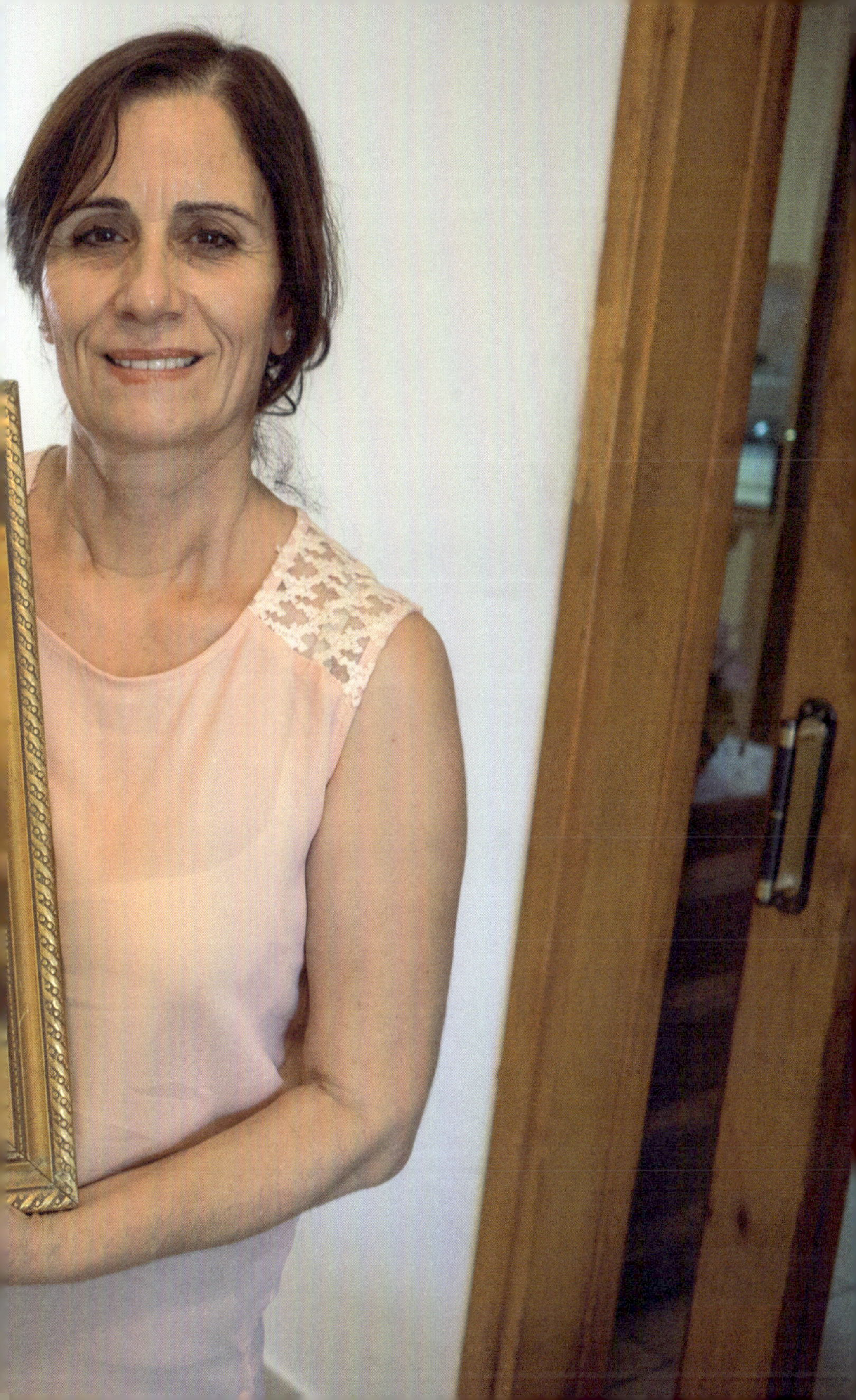

Afterword

Time is Running Out

Now in its tenth year of operation, the CMP has made significant progress in locating and identifying the remains of 2,001 missing persons in Cyprus. The last two years have been the most successful to date. A little over half of the missing persons in Cyprus have now been found and exhumed.

But four to five decades after the events of 1963–64 and 1974, relatives still awaiting news on the fate of their missing are passing away at an ever-increasing rate. Witnesses, whose cooperation is central in locating burial sites, are also dying fast. Hence there is an urgent need for the CMP to accelerate its work.

To achieve this objective, nine bi-communal teams are now excavating across the island every day and investigative efforts are being strengthened, with more investigators seeking to access untapped sources of information such as archives. In addition new technologies such as ground-penetrating radar are being introduced. But these operations are increasingly expensive. Archaeologists face more and more difficulties in locating burial sites, due to the passage of time, topographical changes and the exhaustion of information. Anthropologists are also confronted with more complex cases, necessitating thousands of bone samples every year at a cost of $500 per sample.

Yet the CMP is critical in the search for peace and reconciliation in Cyprus. The need to resolve missing persons cases is more important than ever during the current settlement talks under UN auspices. The recognition of its importance by both communities is reflected in positive developments such as the granting of access to 30 military sites in the north over the next three years.

Over the years the CMP has become a leading institution in the search for, and identification of, missing persons, attracting growing interest from the Middle East, the region where today more people go missing in conflicts than anywhere else in the world. Thus far, in cooperation with the International Committee of the Red Cross and the Argentine Forensic Anthropology Team, the CMP's dedicated scientists have trained 25 Iraqi and 2 Lebanese experts. In addition plans are under way to launch a cooperative programme with Iranian forensic scientists in 2016.

In Cyprus, old wounds that have festered for as long as 50 years are being closed and allowed to heal, thanks to the men and women who support, staff and lead the CMP. This remarkable organisation, one of the island's very few bi-communal institutionalised bodies, must continue to advance humanitarian diplomacy in Cyprus and the region, linking individuals, families and leaders. Their work will heal those wounds and thus contribute towards efforts to foster lasting peace and reconciliation.

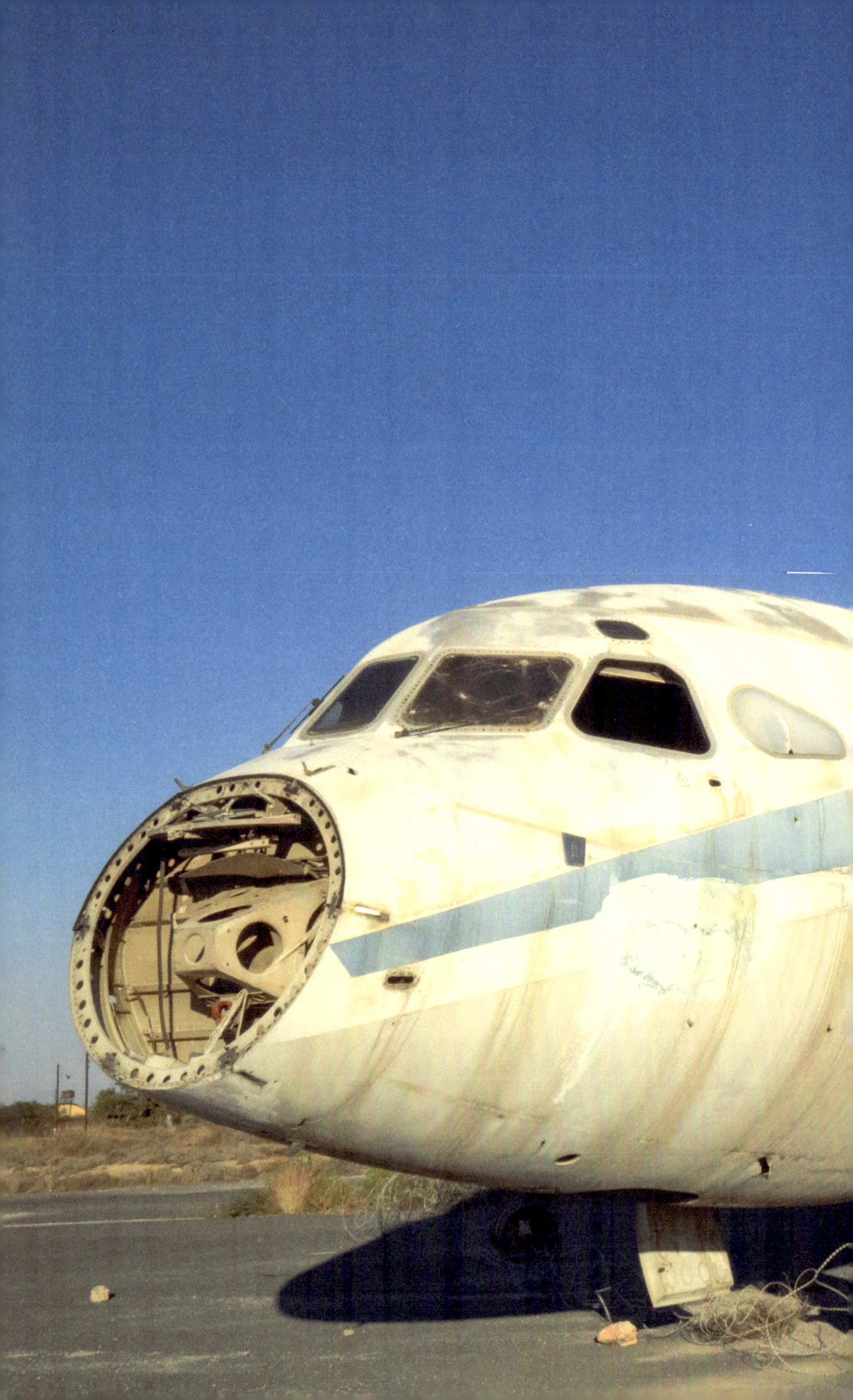

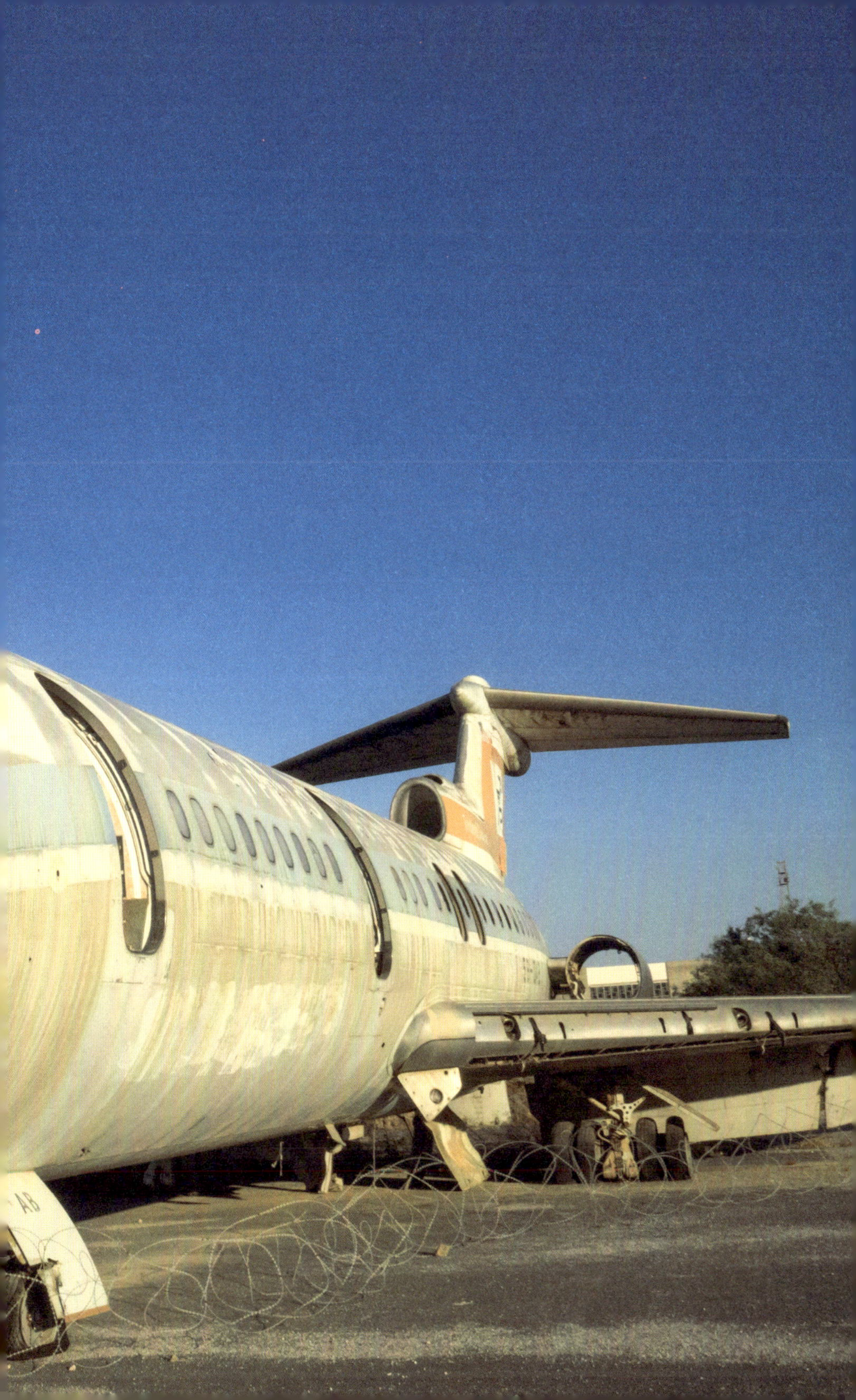
AB

Epilogue by the CMP Members

CMP Members Paul-Henri Arni, Gülden Plümer Küçük and Nestoras Nestoros, left to right, overlooking the old city of Nicosia from the rooftop of the former Ledra Palace Hotel in the UN Buffer Zone, site of their regular meeting place.

I was appointed as the Turkish Cypriot Member of the Committee on Missing Persons in Cyprus in 2006, just before the CMP began the process of exhuming, identifying and returning the remains of missing persons. The CMP is a living project that constantly adapts to needs, scientific developments and realities on the ground. The work of the CMP has changed Cypriots and is in turn shaped by them. Through this project, I have learned how conflict, violence and war can destroy the future of a people; how trauma is passed on to future generations. It is very difficult to heal the trauma of relatives of missing persons, but addressing the issue and bringing closure to a case can help ease the agony of one generation and close the chapter for future generations. We are digging for the past; we do not have answers for everything, but we learn to understand and empathise with the other while doing this work. Addressing a half-century-old problem in the absence of a peace settlement is a unique model. The aim of the CMP to bring closure to families related to events in 1963–64 and 1974 is even more important at a moment where efforts are under way to build a united future for Cypriots. I always wanted to contribute to the peace process in my country. Being part of the CMP is a unique opportunity to promote reconciliation and understanding between the communities in order to build a better future for both Turkish and Greek Cypriots.

Gülden Plümer Küçük, Turkish Cypriot Member

It has been a great privilege for me to participate in this humanitarian effort, although initially I was apprehensive upon taking up this position. Quickly I realized the value of the work and the honour it was to be part of the CMP family, as communicating with relatives revealed that they look upon you as their only hope to find a lost one. You become the solution to the puzzle of hope for their dark anxious bleak years of the past, enabling the missing people to meet up again with their beloved families. For so many years the lives of the relatives of the missing have stood still, leaving them wondering and hoping for the return of their fathers, mothers or children... and finding their remains enables them to attain closure and to move on. The small contribution I have made in this project has been to help and give hope to those who have not only lost all their material assets, being left destitute, but tragically members of their families as well. It gives me tremendous satisfaction to be part of the CMP, that through its activities creates a continuation to the life of the missing person. I also sincerely believe that this work will help heal the scars of the past, bringing greater understanding, breaking dividing lines and bringing hope for lasting peace.

Nestoras Nestoros, Greek Cypriot Member

The CMP recovers, identifies and returns the remains of persons who went missing in Cyprus decades ago. Young Cypriots of both communities carry out this hard work not only for the sake of the dead, but for the sake of the living. In my 23 years with the International Committee of the Red Cross prior to joining the United Nations, I have seen a lot of suffering: people raped during war, tortured in detention, maimed by a landmine, thrown out of their ancestral homes at gunpoint and losing everything they had, including their country. With this experience I can say that the worst wound of war, from which there is no recovery, the only wound that gets worse with time, is when a son, a daughter, a father, a mother, a husband or a wife does not come home for dinner and simply vanishes. We humans are not designed to resist such mental torture. At the political level, if not addressed, the issue of missing persons can be very toxic and can, for decades, stand in the way of reconciliation and political stability between communities and countries. This humanitarian work is therefore critically important even if it is difficult, expensive and time-consuming. It heals individuals, families and communities and gives them back their dignity. It allows countries recovering from violence and war to slowly reconcile with themselves and their neighbours. In Cyprus, the CMP is proud to help families and communities come to terms with the past and to contribute to creating a better future.

Paul-Henri Arni, Third Member (UN)

Beneath the Carob Trees
The Lost Lives of Cyprus

Jointly published in Nicosia in 2016 by Armida Publications and Galeri Kultur Publishing in English, Greek and Turkish, in association with the Committee on Missing Persons in Cyprus (CMP)

No part of this publication may be reproduced or transmitted, in any form or by any means, without prior permission from the publisher and the copyright holder

The views expressed in this book are those of the author and not necessarily those of the CMP or the publishers

ISBN 978-9963-2297-5-8

The CMP wishes to thank the European Union for making this project possible. CMP Members also wish to thank the CMP scientists for telling their story.

Designed by Mark Thomson, London
Set in Garamond Premier Pro
Printed in Belgium by die Keure

Copyright UNDP © 2016
All rights reserved

This project is funded by the European Union